*CMH Pub 104-13

AIRBORNE OPERATIONS
A German Appraisal

For sale by the Superintendent of Documents, U.S. Government Printing Office
Washington, D.C. 20402

Facsimile Edition, 1989

Center of Military History
United States Army
Washington, D.C.

PREFACE

This study was written for the Historical Division, EUCOM, by a committee of former German officers. It follows an outline prepared by the Office of the Chief of Military History, Special Staff, United States Army, which is given below:
1. *a.* A review of German airborne experience in World War II.
    b. An appraisal of German successes and failures.
    c. Reasons for the apparent abandonment of large-scale German airborne operations after the Crete operation.
2. *a.* German experience in opposing Allied and Russian airborne operations.
    b. An appraisal of the effectiveness of these operations.
3. The probable future of airborne operations.

It is believed that the contributors to this study (listed on page iv) represent a valid cross-section of expert German opinion on airborne operations. Since the contributors include Luftwaffe and Army officers at various levels of command, some divergences of opinion are inevitable; these have been listed and, wherever possible, evaluated by the principal German author. However, the opinions of Generalfeld-marschall Albert Kesselring are given separately and without comment wherever they occur in the course of the presentation.

The reader is reminded that publications of the GERMAN REPORT SERIES were written by Germans and from the German point of view. Organization, equipment, and procedures of the German Army and Luftwaffe differ considerably from those of the United States armed forces.

This study is concerned only with the landing of airborne fighting forces in an area occupied or controlled by an enemy and with the subsequent tactical commitment of those forces in conventional ground combat. The employment of airborne units in commando operations, or in the supply and reinforcement of partisans and insurgents, is not included in this study, nor is the shifting of forces by troop-carrier aircraft in the rear of the combat zone. Such movements, which attained large size and great strategic importance during World War II, should not be confused with tactical airborne operations.

THE CONTRIBUTORS

Generalmajor (Brigadier General) Hellmuth Reinhardt, committee chairman and principal author, was Deputy Chief, General Army Office, 1941–43, and later Chief of Staff, Eighth Army, on the southern front in the Ukraine and Romania.

Contributors on German airborne operations:

Generalleutnant (Major General) Werner Ehrig, operations officer of the 22d (Army Air Landing) Division during the attack on Holland.

Oberst (Colonel) Freiherr von der Heydte, an outstanding field commander of German parachute troops, author of the "Appendix."

Generalfeldmarschall (Field Marshal) Albert Kesselring, commander of the German Second Air Force during the Netherlands campaign, and later Commander in Chief, Southwest.

General der Fallschirmtruppen (Lieutenant General) Eugen Meindl, regimental commander during the attack on Crete, later airborne division and corps commander.

Generalleutnant (Major General) Max Pemsel, Chief of Staff, XVIII Corps, which included the ground forces committed in the attack on Crete.

Generaloberst (General) Kurt Student, the chief of German parachute troops during the entire war.

Contributors on Allied airborne operations, and on German defense measures against them:

General der Infanterie (Lieutenant General) Guenther Blumentritt, Chief of Staff, OB West.

Oberst (Colonel) Albert Emmerich, G–3, German First Army.

General der Flakartillerie (Lieutenant General) August Schmidt, in 1944 commander of *Luftgau* VI, which provided the mobile troops to combat Allied airborne landings at Nijmegen and Arnhem.

General der Kavallerie (Lieutenant General) Siegfried Westphal, the chief of staff of OB Southwest in Sicily and Italy, and later of *OB West*.

Oberst (Colonel) Fritz Ziegelmann, G–3, 352d Infantry Division.

FOREWORD*

I concur completely with the ideas of the principal author of this study, which are presented on the basis of his collaboration with the most experienced German specialists.

In view of the present state of technical development, I place a considerably higher estimate on the opportunities for airborne operations in a war between military powers than does the principal author. The latter considers that the essential conditions for the successful use of airborne operations—even on a large scale—exist only in close co-operation with the operations of ground troops.

Assuming that there are sufficiently strong air forces and air transport facilities, I believe that in the future airborne landings by large bodies of troops (several divisions under unified command) can also be used for independent missions, that is, for such military operations as are not closely related in place and time with other ground actions, but are only bound to the latter by the general connections existing between all military operations in a theater of war. It is precisely along these lines that I envisage the future development of airborne warfare. I am convinced that with the proper preparation and present-day technical facilities it is possible to form new military bases by means of large-scale airborne landings far in the enemy's hinterland, in areas where he expects no threat from ground troops and from which independent military operations of large scope can be undertaken. To supply by air such large-scale airheads for the necessary time is essentially a technical problem which can be solved. The independent commitment of large airborne forces seems to offer a present-day high command an effective means for suddenly and decisively confusing the enemy's system of warfare.

Future wars will not be confined to the customary military fronts and combat areas. The battle fronts of opposing ideologies (resistance movements, revolutionary partisan organizations, Irredentist elements), which today in an age of dying nationalism cut through all great powers and civilized nations, will be able to create favorable conditions for large-scale airborne landings deep in the enemy's country and for maintaining such bases of operation as have been won by airborne operations in the interior of the enemy's sovereign territory. To prepare the people in these territories in time and to make them useful in war will be the task of these forces, under a unified command, to which the language of our time has given the name of the "Fifth Column."

---

*By Gen. Franz Halder, Chief of Staff of the German Army, 1938–42.

CONTENTS

	Page
CHAPTER 1. GERMAN AIRBORNE OPERATIONS IN WORLD WAR II	1
Section I. Principles of Employment	2
II. Airborne Tactics	10
III. Parachute Troops	12
IV. Air-Transported Troops	15
V. Troop-Carrier Units	16
VI. Reasons for Success and Failure	17
VII. German Air Landings after Crete	21
CHAPTER 2. ALLIED AIRBORNE OPERATIONS IN WORLD WAR II	25
Section I. Passive Defense Measures	26
II. The German Warning System	27
III. Counterattack in the Air	29
IV. Antiaircraft Defense Fire	29
V. Counterattack on the Ground	30
VI. Counterlanding into the Enemy Airhead	32
VII. An Appraisal of Allied Air Landings	33
VIII. Reflections on the Absence of Russian Air Landings	36
CHAPTER 3. CONCLUSIONS	39
Section I. Evaluation of Past Airborne Experience	39
II. Limitations of Airborne Operations	40
III. Advantages of Airborne Operations	42
IV. Requirements for Success	43
V. Antiairborne Defense	44
VI. Future Possibilities	44
APPENDIX. NOTES ON GERMAN AIRBORNE OPERATIONS	45
Section I. Equipment of German Parachute Troops	45
II. German Employment of Troop-Carrier Units	47
III. Technique and Tactics of Airborne Operations	49

CHAPTER 1
GERMAN AIRBORNE OPERATIONS IN WORLD WAR II

The Germans carried out airborne operations on a large scale only twice in World War II: once in May 1940 in Holland, and again in May 1941 in connection with the occupation of Crete. Accordingly, German experiences are based in the main upon these two operations which took place during the first years of the war and which constituted the first large-scale airborne operations in the history of warfare. Although there were no other major airborne operations launched by the Germans, the German command, and in particular the parachute units which continued to be further improved during the course of the war, seriously concerned themselves with this problem. Two other cases are known in which plans and preparations for large-scale airborne operations progressed very far, namely, the intended commitment of parachute troops as part of the landing in England (Operation SEELOEWE) in 1940, and the preparations for the capture of the island of Malta in 1942. Neither of these plans was carried out.

Airborne operations on a smaller scale were carried out against the Greek island of Leros in 1943 and during the Ardennes offensive in 1944. The experiences of minor operations such as these, as well as the trials, tests, and research done by the airborne troops during the war, are also discussed in this study.

The problems encountered in German airborne operations have been divided into three categories:

1. Planning airborne operations from the point of view of the higher command, designation of objectives for air landings, and co-operation with ground troops, the Luftwaffe, and the naval forces;

2. Actual execution of an airborne operation: the technique and tactics of landing troops from the air; and

3. Organization, equipment, and training.

In addition, a number of specific points and recommendations have been attached in the form of an appendix contributed by Col. Freiherr von der Heydte, who may be regarded as the most experienced field commander of German airborne troops.

In every air landing there are two separate phases. First, a strip of terrain must be captured from the air; that is, an "airhead" must

---

*This publication replaces DA Pam 20-232, October 1951.

be established. This airhead may, or may not, include the objective. Second, the objective of the air landing must either be captured or held in ground battle. The second phase is similar in nature to conventional ground combat, if we disregard the method used to transport the troops and the factors of strength and supply which are influenced by the circumstances that all communication is by air. The first phase, however, has new and unique characteristics. Troops committed during the first phase require special equipment and special training. In limited engagements such troops can also carry out the missions connected with the second phase. For large-scale operations regular ground troops will have to be used in addition to special units. These ground troops need equipment modified to fit the conditions of air transportation.

In recognition of these factors the Wehrmacht (German Armed Forces) had taken two steps even before the war. In the 7th Airborne Division of the Luftwaffe, a unit had been created whose mission it was to capture terrain by parachute jumps and landing troop-carrying gliders. An Army unit, the 22d Infantry Division, had been outfitted for transport by air and given the designation of "Air Landing Division."

Both of these units were committed during the first great air-landing attack in Holland in 1940, at which time the 22d Infantry Division had to be reinforced by elements of the 7th Airborne Division to capture the initial airhead. On the other hand, smaller missions, such as that to capture Fort Eben Emael, were accomplished by troops of the 7th Airborne Division without assistance from other units. During the attack on Crete a year later, it was impossible for the airborne troops to achieve a victory alone. It was only when Army units transported by air had arrived that progress was made toward capturing the island. Since it had not been possible to transport the 22d Infantry Division to Greece in time, the 5th Mountain Division, already in Greece, had to be employed, a measure which proved very successful. Preparations lasting approximately one month were sufficient to prepare the division for the new assignment. The special equipment of the mountain troops was suited both for transport by air and for commitment in the mountainous terrain of the island.

Section I. PRINCIPLES OF EMPLOYMENT

The airborne operations undertaken by the Germans during World War II may be classified in two groups, according to their purpose. In the first group, the attack took the form of sending an advance force by air to take important terrain features, pass obstacles, and hold the captured points until the attacking ground forces arrived. This operation was aimed at a rigidly limited objective within the framework of a ground operation which was in itself essentially limited. This was the case in the airborne operation in Holland in 1940 and, on a smaller scale, at Corinth in 1941 and during the Ardennes offensive in 1944. The common characteristic of all these operations is that they were limited to capturing the objectives and holding them until the ground forces arrived. Beyond that, there was no further action by the troops landed from the air, either in the form of large-scale attacks from the airhead or of independent airborne operations. At the time, such missions would have been far beyond the power of the troops committed.

In the second group are the operations having as their objective the capture of islands. On a large scale these included the capture of Crete in 1941; on a more limited scale, the capture of Leros in 1943. Crete came closer to the concept of an independent operation, although the objective was strictly limited in space. The planned attack on Malta also belongs in this category. The experience of World War II shows that such missions are well within the means of airborne operations. In selecting their objectives even Germany's enemies did not exceed these aims, although they committed substantially greater forces. This does not mean that in the future the objectives of airborne operations cannot be extended.

Two considerations influence the selection of the objective in airborne operations. The first is that in respect to their numbers, and also as far as their type, equipment, and training is concerned, the forces available must be fit for the task facing them. This is of course true of all tactical and strategic planning, but at the beginning of the war, because of a lack of practical experience, the manpower needs were greatly underestimated.

The second consideration—and this is especially important for airborne operations—is that at least temporary and local air superiority is an absolute necessity. This factor has a decisive influence upon the selection of the objective, at least as far as distance is concerned. The latter condition prevailed during the large-scale German airborne operations against Holland and Crete; but the first condition did not exist in equal measure, a fact which led to many crises. Both were absent during the unsuccessful Ardennes offensive.

In preparing for an airborne operation the element of surprise must be maintained. In the operation against Holland surprise was easily achieved since it was the very first time that an airborne operation had ever been undertaken. Once the existence of special units for airborne operations and the methods of commiting them had become known, surprise was possible only through careful selection of time and place for the attack, and of the way in which it was started. This requires strict secrecy regarding preparations. In the Crete operation such secrecy was lacking, and the grouping of parachute troops and transport squadrons became known to the enemy who had little doubt as to their objective. The result was that the German troops landing from the air on Crete came face to face with an enemy ready to defend himself; consequently, heavy losses were sustained.

[Field Marshal Kesselring's comments on the element of surprise:
Airborne operations must always aim at surprise, which has become increasingly difficult but not impossible to achieve. Detection devices, for example radar equipment, can pick up air formations at a great distance and assure prompt countermeasures. Flights at very low altitude, such as were planned for the attack against Malta, are difficult to detect by means of such equipment. The effectiveness of these devices is neutralized by natural barriers in the terrain. Attention can be diverted by deception flights, and confusion is often caused by suddenly changing the course of the aircraft during approach runs, as well as by dropping dummies at various places behind the enemy front. Night operations increase the possibility of surprise; in many cases this is also true for the ensuing ground combat. It is impossible to overestimate the value of soundless glider approaches during twilight hours for the successful execution of air landings. It is easier to preserve secrecy in the assembly of airborne units than in concentrations prior to ground operations of the same size, since with proper organization the airborne troops can be assembled and attacks prepared deep in friendly territory within very short periods of time. Crete is the classic example of how this should *not* be done.] (The Crete operation is discussed in more detail on pages 19 ff.)

Connected with the element of surprise is deception. A typical deceptive measure in airborne operations is the dropping of dummies by parachute. Both sides availed themselves of this measure during World War II. Experience shows that an alert enemy can soon recognize dummies for what they are. A mingling of dummies and real parachutists promises better results because it misleads the enemy as to the number of troops involved and leaves him guessing as to where the point of main effort of the attack is to be located and as to where only a diversionary attack is concerned. As an experiment, the German parachute troops also attempted to equip the dummies with smoke pots which would start smoking when they reached the ground, thus making it still harder for the enemy to see through the deception. This idea never advanced beyond the experimental stage.

Careful reconnaissance is also of special importance in airborne operations. The difficulty is that in airborne operations troops cannot, as in ground combat, conduct their own reconnaissance immediately in advance of the main body of troops. In attacking, their spearheads penetrate country that no reconnaissance patrol has ever trod. This is why reconnaissance will have to be carried out very carefully and well in advance. Military-geographical descriptions, aerial photography, reports from agents, and radio intelligence are sources of information. All this requires time. Before the Holland operation enough time was available, and it was utilized accordingly. Reconnaissance before the Crete attack was wholly inadequate and led to serious mistakes. For instance, enemy positions were described as artesian wells and the prison on the road from Alikaneou to Khania as "a British ration supply depot." Both the command and the troops had erroneous conceptions about the terrain on Crete, all of which could have been avoided if more careful reconnaissance had been made.

Several views were current among German airborne commanders as to the best way of beginning an airborne operation. One method, which General Student recommended and called "oil spot tactics," consisted in creating a number of small airheads in the area to be attacked—at first without any definite point of main effort—and then expanding those airheads with continuous reinforcements until they finally ran together. These tactics were used in both Holland and Crete. General Meindl, on the contrary, was of the opinion that a strong point of main effort had to be built up from the very outset, just as was done in attacks made by the German panzer forces. However, no German airborne operations were launched in accordance with this principle. Neither of the two views can be regarded as wholly right or wrong; which one will prove more advantageous will depend on the situation of one's own and the enemy's forces, terrain, and objective. Even in conventional ground combat an attack based on a point of main effort which has been determined in advance is in opposition to the Napoleonic method of *"on s'engage partout et puis on voit"* (one engages the enemy everywhere, then decides what to do). This implies, however, that a point of main effort will have to be built up eventually by committing the reserves retained for this purpose. If the relatively strong forces required by this method are not available, it would be better to build up a point of main effort from the very beginning. On the other hand, since in airborne operations a thrust is made into terrain where the enemy situation is usually unknown, the "oil spot method" has a great deal in its favor. For example it breaks up enemy countermeasures, as in the attack on Crete. During the initial attack there, parachute troops were distributed in a number of "oil spots"; there were heavy losses and no decisive successes. No further paratroopers were available and the decision was made to land the troop carriers of the 5th Mountain Division wherever an airfield was in German hands, even though it was still under enemy fire. This was taking a great risk, but the plan succeeded from this point onward, the island was captured and the other "oil spots" liberated. At one time, the whole operation was within a hair's breadth of disaster because the airheads, which were too weak and too far apart, were being whittled down. After the decision to attack one point had been carried out and had succeeded, the remaining "oil spots" were useful since they prevented the enemy from moving his forces about freely. The advantages and dangers connected with this method are clear.

The unavoidable inference from the Crete operation is that commanders of airborne troops should land with the very first units so that clear directions for the battle can be given from the outset. The over-all command, however, must direct operations from the jump-off base and influence the outcome by making a timely decision as to where a point of main effort should be built up, and by proper commitment of reserves. For this purpose an efficient communication system and rapid reporting of the situation are necessary.

Since the actual fighting in airborne operations takes place on the ground and in general is conducted in close touch with other ground operations, it is advisable to have both airborne and ground operations under the same command. In the German airborne operations in Crete, the Luftwaffe was in command and neither the ground force commanders in Greece nor the OKH (Army High Command) had anything to do with the preparations; this was a mistake.

In airborne operations the air forces are responsible for keeping the air open for the approach and supply of the landing formations. They also aid in the operation by reconnaissance and by commitment of their tactical formations in preparing the landing and in supporting the troops which have landed. In this they must receive their orders from the command of the ground forces.

[Field Marshal Kesselring's comment on command for airborne operations:

I do not agree with the statement about the conduct of airborne operations. These operations must be considered from the viewpoint of the Armed Forces High Command (OKW). The commander in chief of a theater, for example the Eastern Theater or the Southern Theater, is also a joint forces commander with a joint staff. He is responsible for all airborne operations which are launched within his theater. Hence, the commander of the airborne operation must also be subordinate to him. This commander will generally be an officer of the Air Force whose staff must be supplemented, according to the task assigned him, by Army and Navy officers as well as airborne officers. In some special cases and invariably in those cases where there is no direct connection with the ground and sea fronts, the OKW will plan the operation and conduct it directly. The situation and the mission would probably be the decisive factors in making a decision about the chain of command. If the mission involves supporting a ground attack by means of an airborne operation directly behind the attacked front, the army group will be given the over-all command, will assign missions, and will intervene whenever necessary for the purpose of air-ground co-ordination. As soon as the attacking ground troops establish an effective link-up with the airborne unit, the airborne troops will be brought into the normal chain of command of the attacking ground forces. Unity of command takes precedence over all other considerations. Until that time the airborne troops are commanded by their own unit commanders. The highest ranking officer in the landing area commands at the airhead and is himself subordinate to the commander of the airborne operation—in the above case to the army group commander—who works in close co-ordination with the Air Force commander. In all other cases where, as in Holland, Crete, Oslo, there are no direct connections with operations of the Army or the Navy, a special headquarters, preferably commanded by an Air officer and staffed with Air Force personnel, should be placed in charge of the operation. In appropriate cases, it will be the Air Force commander concerned, especially if the tactical air support units for the airborne operation have to be taken from his sector of the fighting front. This commander's responsibilities include not merely the landing of the first echelon but also the considerably harder problem of directing the following waves and modifying their landing orders in accordance with the development of the situation at the airhead. They also involve the preparatory bombing attack; protection by reconnaissance planes, bombers, and close-support aircraft aimed, I might say, at supporting the ground troops with high and low altitude attacks carried out by the extended arm of a flying artillery; the air transport of supplies; and finally the evacuation by air of casualties, glider pilots, and other specialists. The shortest possible chain of command is decisive for success.]

Mention has already been made of the fact that control of the air is an essential prerequisite for airborne operations. If that control is widespread and based upon maintaining the initiative in air combat, the air support of the airborne force will present few problems. Airborne operations based upon temporary and local air superiority are also possible, but they make strenuous demands upon the attacker's air force. Immediately before an operation, the enemy's forward fighter fields must be rendered useless, and all antiaircraft installations along the route selected for the flight must be neutralized. Enemy radar and communications facilities in the area should also be put out of action, and any enemy reserves near the projected airhead must be subjected to intensive bombardment. Such activity must begin so late that the enemy will have no time to bring in additional troops or to repair the damage.

Each airborne formation will require a fighter escort. From the point of view of air tactics, it will therefore be desirable to keep the number of formations or waves to a minimum. The primary mission of the escort will be to protect the troop-carrier aircraft against enemy fighter planes, especially during the landing and deployment of the troops for ground action. The neutralizing tactics already mentioned will have to be continued during and after the landing to insure the safe arrival of supplies and reinforcements. The troops on the ground will continue to require vigorous air support to take the place of artillery that would normally be supporting them.

Throughout World War II the German parachute troops had the benefit of close co-operation on the part of Luftwaffe reconnaissance. The main problem was to see to it that the parachute troops received good aerial photographs and, if possible, stereoscopic pictures of the area they were to attack so that they could familiarize themselves in advance with the terrain. It proved to be advisable to distribute stereoscopic equipment down to battalion level and to send members of the parachute units to the aerial photography school of the Luftwaffe for special training in the use and interpretation of stereoscopic pictures. In this way, it was possible to offset to a certain degree the lack of terrain reconnaissance prior to an airborne attack.

Finally, the air forces support the airborne operation by attacking the enemy's ground forces. During the war all German airborne operations took place beyond the range of German artillery, and only in the case of the Ardennes offensive were parachute troops to be supported by long-range artillery bombardment. This plan was never put into operation because the radio equipment of the forward observer assigned to the parachute troops failed to function after the jump. Ground strafing and preparatory bombing of the landing area proved to be the best solution everywhere. Air attacks upon enemy reserves being rushed toward the airhead can be of decisive importance because of the extra time gained for the troops which have been landed. Opinions are divided, however, regarding the value of direct air support of the troops fighting on the ground after their landing. On Crete, formations of the Luftwaffe's Von Richthofen Corps solved this problem in exemplary fashion. Other experiences, however, would seem to indicate that it is impossible to support airborne troops, once they are locked in battle, by delivering accurate fire from the air or well-placed bombs. Lack of training and inadequate skill in air-ground co-operation may have disastrous effects. Systematic training, in which well-functioning radio communication from the ground to the air and co-ordination between formations on the ground and in the air are emphasized, should achieve results just as satisfactory as those achieved between armored formations and air forces. It goes without saying that co-operation from the artillery, in so far as airborne operations are conducted within its range, is worth striving for, both in preparation of the landing and in support of the troops after they have landed. Attention may be drawn to the Allied airborne operation north of Wesel in March 1945 where British and American artillery support is said to have been extremely effective. When airborne operations are effected on a beach, naval artillery takes the place of Army artillery. An increase in range made possible by the development of rockets will result in further possibilities for support.

When troops landed by air are joined by forces advancing on the ground, the airborne operation may be said to be terminated. When airborne operations are conducted against islands and coast lines, junction with amphibious forces has the same effect. In World War II, accordingly, airborne operations were always conducted in co-ordination with ground or amphibious forces. How soon this junction with ground or amphibious forces will be effected depends upon the number of troops and volume of supplies, including weapons and equipment, ammunition, rations, and fuel, which can be moved up by air. This again depends upon the air transport available and upon control of the air to insure undisturbed operation of the airlift required for this purpose. If such relief cannot be provided in time, the troops landed will be lost. So far, no way has been devised of fetching them back by air. In the German airborne operations of World War II, supplying troops by air over long periods of time was impossible, not only because control of the air could not be maintained, but also because of a lack of transport planes. In German doctrine, the guiding principle was that as much airlift was needed to resupply a unit which had been landed by air with ammunition and weapons (excluding rations) for a single day of hard fighting as had been necessary for the transport of the unit to the drop point. While this proportion may seem very high and while it may be said that hard fighting does not take place at all times and by all elements at the same time, consideration must be given to the fact that in addition to supplies it will be necessary to bring up more troops to follow up initial successes and give impetus to the fighting. Eventually, the troops will need to be supplied with additional rations and, if they break out of their airhead, with fuel. In this field, too, postwar technical achievements offer new possibilities. During the war the Germans believed that junction of an airborne formation with ground troops had to be effected within two to three days after landing. On the basis of conditions prevailing in those days, these deadlines consistently proved to be accurate in practice.

Section II. AIRBORNE TACTICS

Three methods were used during World War II to land troops from the air at their place of commitment. Troops could be landed by parachute, by transport gliders released from tow planes, or by landing of transport planes. All three methods were used in varied combinations, depending upon the situation. In accordance with the lessons derived from World War II, the last method, for reasons which will be discussed later, is unsuitable for the initial capture of enemy territory from the air, that is, the creation of an airhead. Accordingly, only the commitment of paratroopers and gliderborne troops will be discussed here. (German experiences in the technique and tactics of these two methods are described in detail in the appendix.) The advantages and the disadvantages of the two methods will be compared here and conclusions drawn as to their future use.

Commitment of gliders has the great advantage that they land their whole load in one place. Since debarkation is a matter of seconds, the troops can bring their full fire and striking power to bear immediately after landing. The almost noiseless approach of the gliders, which have been released from the tow planes far from the objective, increases the element of surprise. Furthermore, diving gliders are able to make very accurate spot landings within a limited area. Glider troops are also able to open fire with aircraft armament upon an enemy ready to repulse them. German parachute troops were convinced that this would have an excellent effect on morale. In practice the method was used only once, so far as is known, and that was on a very small scale in July 1944 at Vassieux against the French maquis, but its success was outstanding. While the glider offers pronounced advantages during the first attack on an objective which is defended, in the subsequent phases of the airborne operation its advantages over the use of parachutes lie in the fact that it can deliver substantially greater loads, such as heavy weapons, guns, tanks, and trucks.

On the other hand, parachute jumps make it possible to drop very large numbers of troops at the same time within a certain area. Moreover, until the very last minute the commander can alter his selection of the drop point. He can accordingly adapt himself to changed conditions far more easily than is the case with gliders. The latter are released far from the objective and once this has been done there is no way of changing the landing area.

On this basis it will be seen that the glider is particularly suited for the capture of specifically designated and locally defended objectives, such as Fort Eben Emael, while parachutists are more effective for the purpose of capturing larger areas. Among the German airborne troops a marked preference developed for a method in which an initial attack by gliders was quickly followed up by mass parachute jumps. This plan is not, however, universally applicable. In each case methods will have to be adapted to the situation, terrain, type of objective, and amount of resistance to be expected from the enemy; the commander of the parachute troops will have to make his decision within the framework of his mission.

[Field Marshal Kesselring's comments on the relative merits of parachute and glider landings:

The comparative advantages and disadvantages of parachute and glider landings are well described. Nevertheless, I maintain that at least the same concentration of forces can be achieved with a glider landing as with a parachute jump. Experience shows that parachute landings are very widely scattered, so that assembly takes considerable time. Gliders, according to their size, hold ten to twenty or even more men, who immediately constitute a unit ready for combat. If the landing area is fairly large—the condition of the terrain is of little importance—and if the unit is well trained, the assembly of strong fighting units in a small area will not present any difficulties.]

A weakness in the commitment of gliders is to be found in the fact that once they have been used they are immobilized on the ground and—at least on the basis of German progress by the end of the war—cannot be used twice during the same operation. The German conclusion was that transport planes had to be used as soon as possible. There is no doubt, however, that in time a way will be found to get the gliders back to their base, for example, by the addition of light engines, or the use of helicopters.

[Field Marshal Kesselring's comment on re-use of gliders:

The abandoning of gliders should not be considered a great disadvantage. Their construction is very simple and within the means of even a poor nation. Excessively complicated devices [for glider recovery] should be avoided. But this does not apply to the development of new types of air transport facilities, especially for peacetime and training requirements, which can perhaps also be used in particularly favorable military situations.]

It is important to clear the landing zone immediately so that more gliders can land in their turn. When large-scale glider landings in successive waves are to be made, special personnel will have to be provided for the purpose.

It must be mentioned in this connection that German gliders, patterned on those used in sport, had so-called "breaking points" (*Sollbruchstellen*), that is, joints of purposely weak construction, which would break first in crash landings or collisions with natural or artificial obstacles. This method brought about a substantial economy in construction of the gliders and simplification in procurement of spare parts and maintenance.

Section III. PARACHUTE TROOPS

The necessity of having airborne units for the initial commitment during air landings has been recognized. In both Holland and Crete elements of Army units, in part by design and in part because of ignorance of the situation, were landed from transport planes in territory still occupied by the enemy or situated within sight of enemy artillery observers. This was recognized as a mistake resulting in serious losses. The only thing that saved the planes landing on the Maleme airfield in Crete from being completely destroyed by direct enemy fire was the fact that the ground was covered with dust as a result of drought and that the planes actually landed in clouds of dust.

During the following war years, the parachute troops in Germany were steadily increased and improved. In accordance with the situation and the nature of their intended mission, the troops had to be trained for commitment either by parachute jumps or by transport gliders. The designation of "parachute troops" (*Fallschirmtruppe*) and "parachutists" (*Fallschirmjaeger*) given these units in Germany is accordingly not quite accurate. Fundamentally a major part of the German airborne force was suited for transport-glider commitment only, since the plans of training them as parachutists could not be carried out. In practice, the percentage of trained parachutists steadily decreased with the result that, as the war continued, these troops were almost exclusively used in ground combat. The Wehrmacht, because of the scarcity of manpower, found it impossible to keep these units in reserve for their special duties. It is evident that only the "rich man" can afford such forces, and that efforts must be made to withdraw these troops as soon as possible after each airborne commitment. Otherwise their value as special units will rapidly decrease, something very hard to remedy.

One fundamental lesson derived from the first air landing was that even the very first elements reaching the ground must be fully equipped for battle. The parachutists landing on Crete had nothing but their pistols and hand grenades, the remaining weapons and ammunitions being dropped separately in special containers. After the Crete operation this was changed. It was realized that both parachute and transport glider troops must reach the ground as combat units ready for action. They must have heavy weapons, and especially, tank-destroying weapons, adapted to this type of transportation, as well as a suitable type of organization for even the smallest units, making it possible for each to fight independently. (Detailed information regarding the equipment of German parachute troops is contained in the appendix.) In order to capture a usable airhead for the air-transported units, the parachute troops, over and above the initial landing, must be able to capture airfields, or at least terrain suitable for landing air transports, and to push back the enemy far enough from these areas to avoid the necessity of landing within range of direct enemy gunfire. In other words, the parachute troops must be capable of attacks with a limited objective, and of holding the captured terrain. Consequently, the parachute divisions were equipped with all heavy weapons and artillery; and an airborne panzer corps was organized with one panzer and one motorized infantry division. However, organization of these units never got beyond the initial activation as conventional ground troops, and all plans to use them for airborne landings remained in the theoretical stage. After the Crete operation no German parachute division was committed in airborne operations as a whole unit. The airborne panzer corps never even received adequate training. Only parts of the remaining parachute divisions, of which there were six in 1944 and ten or eleven at the end of the war in 1945, were trained for airborne operations. General Student gives a total figure of 30,000 trained parachutists in the summer of 1944. Most of them were in the 1st and 2d Parachute Divisions, of whose personnel 50 and 30 percent respectively were trained parachutists. Commitment of the divisions in ground combat continually decreased these figures so that parachutists from all units had to be recruited for the airborne attack in the Ardennes offensive. In the main, the training of these troops was inadequate. For instance, only about 20 percent of the parachutists committed in this action were capable of jumping fully equipped with weapons. This was a serious disadvantage because very few of the weapons containers dropped were recovered.

Accordingly, the Germans had no practical experience in large-scale commitment of parachutists with really modern equipment, nor was it possible to test the organization and equipment of such formations in actual combat.

Earlier German experience points to two important considerations. In the first place, the parachute troops will be in need of a supply service immediately after landing. On the basis of the Crete experience, it would seem advisable to incorporate service units in the first waves of parachutists. The greater the scale of the airborne operation, the more thought will have to be given to the matter of motorized supply vehicles. Today their transportation in transport gliders presents no technical difficulties. In the second place, in cases where the intention is to follow up initial jumps with the landing of great numbers of air-transported troops, engineer units will have to be assigned to the parachute troops at an early stage for the purpose of preparing and maintaining landing strips for transport planes.

Even though the German parachute troops lost their actual purpose in the last years of the war, they preserved their specific character in the organization of their personnel replacements. The operations actually carried out proved that the special missions assigned to parachute troops call for soldiers who are especially aggressive, physically fit, and mentally alert. In jumping, the paratrooper must not only conquer his own involuntary weakness but upon reaching the ground must be ready to act according to circumstances; he must not be afraid of close combat; he must be trained in the use of his own and the enemy's weapons; and, finally, his will to fight must not be impaired by the privations occasioned by such difficulties in supply as hunger, thirst, and shortage of weapons. For this reason, it is advisable for the parachute troops to take their replacements primarily from among men who have volunteered for such service. The excellent quality of the replacements which the German parachute troops were able to obtain until the very end explains why, even in ground combat, they were able to give an especially good account of themselves.

Good replacements, however, require careful training in many fields. Every paratrooper must be given thorough training in infantry methods, especially in close combat and commando tactics. This was shown to be necessary in all the operations undertaken. Only when the paratrooper proves from the outset to be superior to the attacking enemy can he be successful. Specialist training in the use of various arms and special techniques is essential. A mistake was made by the Germans in separating the initial jump training from the rest of the training program. Instead of becoming the daily bread of the paratrooper, jump practice accordingly evolved into a sort of "special art." All artificiality must be avoided in this branch of training.

Special emphasis must be placed on training officers for the parachute troops. One of the experiences derived from actual operations is that the officers must be past masters in the art of ground combat. The fact that the German parachute troops originated in the Luftwaffe caused a great many inadequacies in this respect. On the other hand, the parachute officer must have some knowledge of aviation, at least enough to be able to assess the possibilities of airborne operations.

There is no doubt that a sound and systematic training program for the parachute troops demands a great deal of time and that in the last years of the war the German parachute formations no longer had this time at their disposal. However, the time required for training, combined with the high standards set for the selection of replacements, acts as a deterrent to their commitment. The higher command will decide to make use of the troops only when all preconditions for a great success are at hand or when necessity forces it to do so. To commit these troops in regular ground combat is a waste. Commitment of parachute divisions in ground combat is justified only by the existence of an emergency. Once the divisions are committed as ground troops they lose their characteristic qualities as specialists.

Section IV. AIR-TRANSPORTED TROOPS

The original German plan to use Army troops for this purpose and to equip and train them accordingly was abandoned early in the war. The 22d Infantry Division, which had been selected in peacetime for the purpose, participated in airborne operations only once, in Holland in 1940. It was found that their double equipment—one set for regular ground combat, the other for use in air-landing operations—constituted an obstacle; consideration for their special mission limited their employment for ground combat. When a fresh commitment in line with their special mission became a possibility in Crete, it was found impossible to bring them up in time. On the other hand, as early as the Norway campaign, mountain troops were flown for commitment at Narvik without much prior preparation. While in this case nontactical transport by air was involved, the previously mentioned commitment in 1941 of the 5th Mountain Division in the airborne operation against Crete took place after only short preparation and was entirely successful.

On the basis of these experiences the idea of giving individual Army units special equipment for airborne operations was abandoned. The German High Command set about finding ways and means to adapt *all* Army units for transport by air with a minimum of changes in their equipment. The results were never put into practice because after Crete the Germans did not undertake any other airborne operations on a large scale. Crete, however, proved that the German mountain troops, because of their equipment and the training which they had received, as well as their combat methods, were particularly suited for missions of this nature. In the future the goal must be to find a way of committing not only mountain and infantry divisions but panzer and motorized formations in airborne operations. Their equipment and organization for this purpose will depend upon the evaluation of technical possibilities which cannot be discussed in detail here. The chief demand which the military must make upon the technical experts is that the changes required for such commitment be kept to a minimum. A way must be found to determine the best method for such a change so that the troops can undertake it promptly at any time.

The lesson learned from German airborne operations in World War II was that air-transported troops can be committed only if the success of landing and unloading is guaranteed by a sufficiently large landing zone. These troops are not suited to the purpose of capturing an airhead. With the exception of the technical details concerned with their enplaning, these troops require no special training. The logical conclusion to be drawn from this lesson is that parachute troops, who capture the airhead, must be increased in number and supplied with more fire power.

Section V. TROOP CARRIER UNITS

Transporting troops by air to their area of commitment is more or less a matter of transportation alone and in an efficiently organized modern air force presents no difficulty at all. However, the approach flight and dropping of parachute troops is a part of the operation itself and determines its subsequent success or failure. The inconclusive but rather disappointing German experiences in this field have been set down, from the point of view of an airborne field commander, in the appendix. Transport squadrons—including both the transport planes for the parachutists and the tow planes for the gliders—are to the parachute troops what horse teams are to the artillery and motor vehicles to the motorized forces. In each case correct tactical leadership for each mode of transport is a prerequisite for the correct commitment of the troops in time and space—consequently, they must be trained jointly. During commitment the transport squadrons must be subordinated to the parachute commanders, who must be trained to give orders to the transport squadrons in correct and systematic form. The ideal solution would undoubtedly be to incorporate the transport squadrons organically into the airborne forces, but this solution is expensive. Lack of sufficient matériel alone made it impracticable during World War II as far as the Wehrmacht was concerned. A compromise solution would be close co-operation in peacetime training. The transport squadrons will have to be made available to the parachute units well in advance of an airborne operation since joint rehearsals are a prerequisite of success. This fact increases the amount of time needed for the preparation of an airborne operation and at the same time endangers the secrecy surrounding the undertaking, because such a grouping of units can give the enemy valuable leads regarding one's intentions.

The most important factor is the selection of the time and place of the jump and of the release of the gliders. This requires very precise orders and is subject to the decision of the commander of the parachutists. Again and again lack of care in this regard resulted in breakdowns during German airborne operations in World War II. Only twice did strict observance of this point result in smooth functioning—during the airborne operations to capture the Isthmus of Corinth in 1941, when the limited scope of the undertaking made it possible to commit transport squadrons having just finished thorough training in co-operation with parachutists; and during the capture of Fort Eben Emael in 1940, when the units participating in the operation had received joint training over an extended period.

The principle of subordinating the transport squadrons to the parachute commanders makes it imperative that the training of these commanders be extended to include flight training.

In this connection mention must be made of the so-called pathfinder airplanes, whose mission in relation to airborne operations at night is described in the appendix. What has been said above also holds good for them. Their proper use is essential for success and demands, above all, skill in navigation in order to calculate timing accurately.

Section VI. REASONS FOR SUCCESS AND FAILURE

In assessing the successes and failures of German airborne operations the following missions are taken into consideration: Holland, 1940; Corinth, 1941; Crete, 1941; Leros, 1943; and Ardennes, 1944. All other commitments of German airborne troops fall into the category of commando operations or of troop movements by air.

Holland, 1940.—On the whole, the airborne operations against Holland, in spite of a number of critical moments and relatively great losses, must be classified as successful. This success was connected not so much with achievement of the tactical objectives, such as the capture of a number of bridges which were important to the attacking ground forces, as with the morale influence exerted upon the enemy by a wholly new method of fighting. The very fact that in this way large forces could penetrate deep behind Dutch defenses at the outset of the fighting undoubtedly broke the resistance of the Dutch and saved the German Army the cost of a serious fight in capturing Holland. Success is attributable mainly to the surprise provoked by this method, which was used for the first time in the history of warfare.

[Field Marshal Kesselring's comments on airborne operations in Holland:

This was the first airborne operation in history and should be treated in somewhat greater detail. The operation was under the over-all direction of the commander of Second Air Force. The tactical commander was General Student. His headquarters was divided into a mobile forward echelon, headed by Student in person, and a stationary rear echelon, which was to assume special importance.

The operation was divided into the following parts:

1. An operation with gliders alone against Fort Eben Emael and the Maas bridge. With the capture of Fort Eben Emael, the enemy flanking actions against the Maas crossings were eliminated. The capture of the most important bridge guaranteed that the Maas River would be crossed according to plan and thus established the necessary conditions for the co-ordination of ground and air operations in Holland. The dawn missions succeeded surprisingly well.
2. A major airborne operation by two divisions to capture the Moordijk bridges, the Rotterdam airport, the city of Rotterdam, and the Dutch capital of The Hague and its airfields. Since the second part of the mission (22d Infantry Division—The Hague) was not successful, the subsequent operations in the Dutch coastal area failed to take place.

The attempt at surprise was successful. Today one cannot even imagine the panic which was caused by rumors of the appearance of parachutists, supported by the dropping of dummies, etc. Nevertheless, the surrender of Rotterdam was the result of the bold actions of the parachutists and the air attack against the defended positions in Rotterdam. The operation had been organized by Student with the thoroughness characteristic of him. In fact, it had been a small military masterpiece, particularly with respect to the following:

a. The deployment of troops and troop-carrier formations among the only airfields near the border, just within range of the most distant objectives.

b. The incorporation of escort fighter wings in the transport movement, for which General Osterkamp can claim both the responsibility and the credit.

c. The co-ordination of the bomber escort attacks with the landing operations, which had been rendered even more difficult because the commander in chief of the Luftwaffe had ordered an attack against reported enemy naval vessels on the previous evening.

The success of the airborne operation with respect to its strategic effect is incontestable. The Dutch Theater of Operations was practically eliminated. The failures and losses can be attributed to the following:

a. Interference with the plan of attack by the commander in chief of the Luftwaffe, mentioned above.

b. The inadequate strength of parachutists in the air attack group of the 22d Infantry Division.

c. Defects in co-ordination between the 22d Infantry Division and the troop-carrier formations and inadequate training of both in the tactical doctrine for carrying out an airborne operation.

d. Technical defects in the signal communications system which made it diffcult or impossible for the parachutists and transport formations to co-operate with the 22d Infantry Division and, similarly, hampered General Student in issuing orders to that division.

e. The command technique of General Student, who thought of himself as the commander of the Rotterdam operation and thus neglected liaison with the Second Air Force, especially during the most decisive hours.

However, all in all, the airborne operation proved successful as the first of its kind because essentially it was correctly organized and carried out with unparalleled verve. It taught us a great number of practical lessons, the application of which did not present any problems which were insurmountable from a technical or tactical point of view. It proved that an airborne operation needs its own command posts, both on the ground and in the air, as well as representation at a higher level.]

Corinth, 1941.—This was an operation on a limited scale undertaken by well-trained parachute troops and troop-carrier units. Resistance was limited. As far as execution of the operation is concerned, it may be rated as a complete success. The actual tactical success was limited to capture of the Isthmus of Corinth. The bridge over the Corinth Canal was destroyed by an explosion of undetermined origin, but makeshift repairs made it possible to use the bridge again that same day. If the attack had been made a few days earlier, the airborne operation, in the form of a vertical envelopment, could have been far more successful and large numbers of the British Expeditionary Force could have been cut off from access to their embarkation ports on the Peloponnesus. It is true, however, that resistance would have been greater in this case.

Crete, 1941.—The capture of the island of Crete was the most interesting and most eventful German airborne operation. The initial attack contained all the germs of failure. Only the fact that the defenders of the island limited themselves to purely defensive measures and did not immediately and energetically attack the landing troops saved the latter from destruction. Even though the situation was still obscure, the German command decided to commit its reserves (5th Mountain Division) in an all-out attack against the point which seemed to offer the greatest chances of success; the energetic, purposeful, and systematic commitment of these forces in an attack immediately after their landing changed the threatened failure into a success. A serious disadvantage for the attackers was British control of the sea at the beginning of the operation. Only after several days was it possible to break down this control to such an extent that somewhat insecure communications with the island were possible.

[Field Marshal Kesselring's comments on airborne operations in Crete:

I did not participate in the Crete operation, but later was frequently in Crete, and I have also talked with many parachute officers who were in action there.

The special characteristic of this operation was its improvisation. That the objective of the operation was achieved so quickly, in spite of all reverses, is the greatest tribute which can be paid to the fighting men and commanders engaged in it. Improvisation, however, should be avoided if possible, since the risk involved is too high in proportion to the number of men committed. But it is not true, as stated in this report, that "an airborne operation is . . . time consuming . . . and affords neither much freedom of maneuver nor a great deal of flexibility." (See page 43.)

If the airborne troops have a suitable, permanent organization and if reconnaissance is begun early and carried out with all available means, there is no reason for assuming that an airborne operation cannot be carried out as swiftly as the situation demands. The art of command lies in thinking ahead. Applied to this particular problem, this means the prearrangement of an adequate, efficient ground organization, such as was available in the case of Crete, and the timely procurement of the necessary fuel, etc., via land or sea, which would also have been possible. Under ideal conditions, if permanent large-scale airborne formations had been available, this would have presented even fewer difficulties, since the combat troops would have been flown in by their own transport planes. One can easily conclude from this that a high degree of surprise might have been achieved under the assumed conditions. I repeat, because of the elements of danger inherent in airborne operations, improvisations can be resorted to only in exceptional cases and under particularly favorable conditions. Otherwise they should be rejected.

In this case it would have been advisable for the commander of the airborne operation and, if possible, the division commanders to have made a personal reconnaissance flight to inform themselves about terrain conditions and possible defense measures of the enemy, as a supplement to the study of photographs. The exceptionally unfavorable landing conditions should have induced them to land in a single area away from the occupied objectives with their effective defense fire, and then to capture the decisive points (airport and seaport) intact in a subsequent conventional infantry attack at the point of main effort. In doing this it would not have been necessary to abandon the use of surprise local glider landings directly into key points, the possession of which would have facilitated the main attack.]

Leros, 1943.—This was an operation on a limited scale which, in spite of some inadequacies in execution, led to success within four days, mainly as a result of a favorable situation and co-ordination with landings from the sea. (See also pages 47 and 48.)

Ardennes, 1944.—The airborne operations connected with the Ardennes offensive were definitely a failure. The force committed was far too small (only one battalion took part in the attack); the training of parachute troops and troop-carrier squadrons was inadequate; the Allies had superiority in the air; the weather was unfavorable; preparations and instructions were deficient; the attack by ground forces miscarried. In short, almost every prerequisite of success was lacking. Therefore, it would be wrong to use this operation as a basis for judging the possibilities of airborne operations. At that time the Wehrmacht was so hopelessly inferior to the enemy in manpower and matériel that this operation can hardly be justified and is to be regarded only as a last desperate attempt to change the fortunes of war.

Section VII. GERMAN AIR LANDINGS AFTER CRETE

The airborne operation against Crete resulted in very serious losses which in percentage greatly exceeded those sustained by the Germans in previous World War II campaigns. The parachute troops were particularly affected. Since everything Germany possessed in the way of parachute troops had been committed in the attack on Crete and had been reduced in that campaign to about one-third of their original strength, too few qualified troops remained to carry out large-scale airborne operations at the beginning of the Russian campaign. Air transportation was also insufficient for future operations.

Furthermore, the German High Command had begun to doubt whether such operations would continue to pay—the Crete success had cost too much. The parachute troops themselves, however, recovered from the shock. Their rehabilitation was undertaken and lessons were drawn from the experience, so that a year later a similar undertaking against the island of Malta was energetically prepared.

At this point, however, Hitler himself lost confidence in operations of this nature. He had come to the conclusion that only airborne operations which came as a complete surprise could lead to success.

After the airborne operations against Holland and Crete, he believed surprise attacks to be impossible and maintained that the days of successful airborne operations were over. The fact that the Cretan operations came so close to defeat strengthened his opinion. Moreover, the Malta operation would have to be prepared in Italy and launched from there. Prior experience with the Italians had proved that the enemy would be apprised in advance regarding every single detail of the preparations, so that even a partial surprise was impossible. Since Hitler had no confidence at all in the combat value of the troops, which with the exception of the German parachute troops were to be of Italian origin exclusively, he did not believe the undertaking could be successful and abandoned its execution. The special circumstances prevailing at that time may have justified this particular decision, but the basic attitude in regard to airborne operations later turned out to be wrong.

According to General Student, Hitler and the commander in chief of the Luftwaffe were so thoroughly convinced that the days of successful airborne operations were over that they believed that not even the enemy would engage in any more large-scale preparations for airborne operations. When the attack by British and American paratroopers on Sicily proved the contrary, the Wehrmacht was itself no longer in a position to carry out large-scale airborne operations. The main essential, superiority in the air, was lacking. The Luftwaffe, no longer a match for the Allied air forces, was unable to assemble enough planes to attain the necessary local superiority in the air and to maintain it for the time required; nor was the Luftwaffe able to make available sufficient transport space. It is true that airborne units were available, but because manpower was so scarce they were constantly being committed in ground operations. The special nature of their mission was retained only to the extent that they were transported by air to points that were threatened and that in some cases, as in Sicily, they were also dropped by parachute. Aside from this, their training in their special fields suffered from a lack of aircraft required for the purpose.

At the time of the Allied invasion of France the commander in chief of the Luftwaffe proposed to link up the planned counterattack with airborne operations in force. The OKW turned him down because first, the parachute troopers available were already fighting on the ground; second, their training was inadequate for such a purpose; and third, even if the needed troop carriers could be provided, the hopeless inferiority of the Luftwaffe made it impossible to achieve control of the air either in space or in time.

The lesson based upon German operations may then be summarized as follows: In airborne operations cheap successes cannot be achieved with weak forces by means of surprise and bluff. On the contrary, airborne operations which are to achieve success on a large scale require a great outlay of matériel, outstanding personnel, and time for training and preparation. Such operations are accordingly "expensive." From 1941 on Germany, in comparison to its enemies, was "poor."

CHAPTER 2

ALLIED AIRBORNE OPERATIONS IN WORLD WAR II

The following discussion is based mainly on three major airborne operations in western Europe—Normandy in June 1944 (the invasion), Nijmegen and Arnhem in September 1944, and north of Wesel in March 1945. The author had little data at his disposal concerning the actions against Allied airborne operations in Sicily in 1943, but this will hardly impair the validity of the following statements, since the airborne landings in western Europe as well as the defense against them were based on lessons of the Sicilian campaign. Any analysis of these operations will therefore cover by implication the earlier experiences in Sicily, so far as they have not been superseded by more recent information.

[Field Marshal Kesselring's comments on Allied airborne operations in Sicily:

The first Allied airborne operations in Sicily preceded the American and British landings by sea. After jumping, the parachutists were scattered over a wide and deep area by the strong wind. Operating as nuisance teams, they considerably impeded the advance of the Hermann Goering Panzer Division and helped to prevent it from attacking the enemy promptly after the landings at Gela and elsewhere. This opposition would not have made itself felt so strongly if General Conrath had not organized his troops in march groups contrary to correct panzer tactics.

The second airborne operation of British parachutists took place in the night of 13–14 July 1943, close to the Simeto bridge on the highway between Catania and Lentini. The Commander in Chief, South (*OB SUED*) anticipated an airborne operation in the Catania plain, even if an amphibious landing were not attempted there. He therefore had ordered that those parts of the plain which were west of the Catania airfield be denied the enemy through installation of wooden obstacles. The antiaircraft units protecting the large airfields in the Catania plain had been specially charged with defense against airborne troops. During the first day of the landing operation, every Allied air landing in the area around Catania could be attacked from the north by reserves of Brigade Schmalz of the Herman Goering Panzer Division and by troops of the 1st Parachute Division, which had been flown in to the eastern coast of Sicily. Even assuming the most favorable conditions for the enemy parachutists, no great Allied success could be expected, at least no success which justified such a large commitment of men. Thus it was inevitable that the British parachute attack in the night of 13–14 July 1943 was crushed. Even their purely tactical success in occupying the Simeto bridge was only of a temporary nature and had no effect on the over-all situation.]

Section I. PASSIVE DEFENSE MEASURES

The great latitude which the airborne attacker enjoys in selecting his target makes it extremely difficult for the defender to take passive defense measures against airborne operations. It is quite impossible to set up antiair-landing obstacles throughout the country. Therefore, no more can be done than to determine what might constitute particularly desirable targets for an airborne attack and in what specific areas air landings directed against these targets might be undertaken by the enemy. These principles were followed by Germany in taking defensive measures against an invasion in the West, since experience in Sicily clearly indicated that the enemy would also resort to airborne operations during an invasion. Accordingly, German antiairborne measures were determined by the following two aims: first, to render useless any points which appeared particularly well suited for landing operations; and secondly, to protect all likely targets against attack by airborne troops.

The first purpose was served by erecting posts approximately 10 feet long and 6 to 8 inches in diameter, imbedded 3 feet deep, connected by wires, and partly equipped with demolition charges. These obstacles were intended to prevent the landing of troop-carrying gliders. German experience showed that such post obstacles are effective only if they are equipped with demolition charges. If no demolition charges are used, although the glider may crash, the enemy will still be able to make a successful landing.

Mining and flooding the terrain were additional measures. The former can be effective against gliders as well as airborne troops if the enemy lands at the very point where the mine field has been laid. However, since such mine fields are necessarily limited because of shortage of matériel and personnel, it is really a matter of luck if the enemy happens to land in a mine field. Furthermore, in the interest of one's own troops, the local inhabitants, and agriculture and forestry, it is impossible to consider extensive application of this method. Undoubtedly, flooding large areas by means of artificial damming deters the enemy from landing at the particular spots. This method, in addition to others, was widely used on the Atlantic coast. Unfortunately, however, at the time of the invasion, some of these flooded areas had dried up again because of lack of rain.

Laying mine fields and flooding areas serve a twofold purpose if, by their location, they not only prevent airborne landings but at the same time constitute obstacles against attack on the ground.

In order to protect potential targets, preparations were made for all-around defense by establishing fortifications, obstacles, and barriers and by wiring bridges for demolition. These are measures which have to be taken everywhere in modern warfare—not only against airborne operations but also against penetrations by mobile forces on the ground, against commando raids, and in occupied territories against partisans and rebels. Wherever they were adequately prepared and reinforced by the necessary personnel, they served their purpose.

Orders for resistance against invasion on the Atlantic coast called for an inflexible defense in which the coast constituted the main line of resistance. To counter any simultaneous large-scale airborne operations, instructions were issued to develop a "land front" several miles inland, with its rear to the coast. In this manner, it was intended to establish a fortified area between "ocean front" and "land front" which was to be defended like a fortress, thus preventing the juncture of the enemy elements attacking from the sea and those landing inland from the air. During the invasion, however, the Allies did not oblige by landing their troops inland beyond the land front, but landed them either into it or between the two fronts. Furthermore, since the German land front was occupied by insufficient forces because of a shortage of personnel and since it had not been adequately developed, its value was illusory. As a matter of fact, the obstacles, such as the flooding, at some points even protected Allied airborne troops against attacks by German reserves.

Experience taught the Germans that passive measures have a limited value against airborne operations. Furthermore, in view of the great amount of time and matériel required, they can be employed only where the fronts are inactive for a long period of time. In mobile warfare, the only passive measures to be applied are preparations for an all-around defense carried out by all troops, staffs, supply services, etc., behind the lines.

Section II. THE GERMAN WARNING SYSTEM

The prerequisite for a successful defense against enemy airborne operations is the early recognition of preparations for such operations. Frequently the signs of imminent air landings may be recognized from agents' reports and radio interception. The Germans themselves had no doubt that the invasion from the West would involve airborne operations on a large scale. On the other hand, it will nearly always remain uncertain up to the last moment, where and when these operations may take place. Changes in the over-all picture obtained through radio interception may appear to give advance warning of an attack. If such changes occur frequently without an actual operation taking place, the alertness of the defender becomes blunted.

The first positive reports are obtained through radar detection of the approach flight. In one case in Normandy it was possible, on the basis of radar, to infer as early as two hours before the jump that an airborne formation was approaching, and to alert the German forces in time.

A well-organized observation service based on the co-operation of all units and agencies, even in the rear areas, should provide assurance that the point where enemy forces are actually landing is quickly determined. All observation, however, is useless unless the reports are rapidly transmitted to the superior agencies and to units immediately concerned. Experience has proved that telephone communications are unreliable for this purpose since they are frequently disrupted by enemy action, such as preparatory bombing attacks. The transmittal of prepared messages by radio and appropriate warning broadcasts which all agencies and troops are able to receive has proved effective.

As soon as the air landings are an established fact, the next step is to determine where they are concentrated, which of the attacks are being made for the purpose of diversion and deception, and how wide an area is covered. This is extremely difficult, especially at night, and usually considerable time passes before some degree of clarity is possible. Therein lies the defender's greatest weakness. However, it is never advisable to delay countermeasures until this clarity has been obtained. In most cases, the situation will remain obscure until the counterattack is launched. It is all the more important, therefore, that reporting should not be neglected during the fighting; this is a matter of training and indoctrination.

It is a unique characteristic of airborne operations that the moments of greatest weakness of the attacker and of the defender occur simultaneously. The issue is therefore decided by three factors: who has the better nerves; who takes the initiative first; and who acts with greater determination. In this connection, the attacker always has the advantage of being free to choose the time and place of attack, and he therefore knows in advance when the moment of weakness will occur, whereas the defender must wait to find out where and when the attack will take place.

The attacker will always endeavor to aggravate the defender's disadvantages by deception and try to force him to split up his countermeasures. As already mentioned in Chapter 1, the most popular method of deception is the dropping of dummies with parachutes. In such cases an immediate attack rapidly determines whether it is a genuine landing operation or a diversion. Radio interception will also prove to be helpful at an early stage, for troops just landed must make prompt use of radio communications to establish contact with each other and with their superior commands at the jump-off base. Radio, however, cannot be used in diversionary actions. Even if dummies were equipped with radio sets functioning automatically or by remote control—which should not be an insoluble technical problem—alert and competent radio interception personnel would not be deceived for long. During the invasion in 1944, it was the signal intelligence service which was able, with comparative rapidity, to give the high command an accurate picture of the enemy's tactical grouping during the air landings. The attacker will naturally endeavor to eliminate any targets such as radar equipment and long-distance radio stations by air attacks prior to the air landings. On the other hand, such attacks can also be an advance warning for the defender.

In occupied territories it is also possible by careful observation and surveillance of underground activities to discover indications of imminent air landings, particularly if counterespionage elements succeed in infiltrating the enemy's network of agents.

Section III. COUNTERATTACK IN THE AIR

Theoretically, the defender's best method of defense against air landings is the employment of air forces to attack the enemy while he is still approaching and to annihilate him or force him to turn back. In 1944–45 during the Western campaign, it was a foregone conclusion that victories were out of the question in view of the hopeless inferiority of the Luftwaffe. To repeat, mastery of the air by the attacking air force will always be the prerequisite for successful airborne operations. The attacker endeavors, by means of bombing attacks, to destroy the defender's air forces on the ground and to protect the approach flight with superior numbers of escort fighters. If the attacker is unable to accomplish this, he will of necessity abandon the idea of an airborne operation altogether. Only in exceptional cases and under particularly favorable conditions will it be possible for the defender to launch an air attack against approaching air formations with any chance of success.

Section IV. ANTIAIRCRAFT DEFENSE FIRE

A report made in June 1944 by Army Group B on the battle of Normandy includes the following statement: "The designation of areas to be taken under fire by all weapons while opposing the landing of airborne troops has proved satisfactory. (Fire by 20-mm. guns directed at enemy landing forces proved to be particularly effective.)" Countermeasures taken by the attacker include landings at night or during poor visibility. In this connection, the same report says, "Rainy weather and low clouds are favorable for airborne operations, because planes are able to dive and land without being hit by flak."

It is undoubtedly advisable to inflict the highest possible losses on airborne troops while they are still in the air and while they are landing. To this end, it is necesary for all weapons within whose range an enemy plane is landing to take such a plane under fire. At Arnhem the British troops that landed in the vicinity of the Deelen airfield suffered heavy losses inflicted by German antiaircraft fire. By the same token, however, it is true that antiaircraft fire alone cannot succeed in preventing an air landing, since enemy troops descending by parachute cannot be held off or turned back by overwhelming fire, as might be the case during ground combat. They have to come down, whether they want to or not, and some of them will always succeed in reaching the ground in good fighting condition. It would be a mistake to say on that account that antiaircraft defense fire offers no chance of success. On the contrary, it is the very moment of landing which holds out the greatest promise of success for antiaircraft defense, for the enemy troops which are landing are without cover; they are defenseless to a certain degree and likely to suffer very heavy casualties. At this juncture, it is impossible for the attacker to protect the troops from the air or by long-range artillery fire. Only gliders can use their arms against the firing defenders, and then only if they happen to be landing at the appropriate diving angle. The losses suffered by airborne troops while jumping and landing will greatly impair their combat efficiency and power of resistance. This will facilitate the task of subsequently annihilating them, and thus frustrate the landing attempt. For instance, the German invasion of Crete illustrates that it is possible to inflict serious casualties by antiaircraft fire. The same example, however, also demonstrates that the employment of antiaircraft fire alone is not sufficient to effectively resist an invasion. It can be achieved only through attack. If the defenders of Crete had not contented themselves with using antiaircraft fire alone but had immediately attacked the troops which had landed, the entire invasion would have failed at the outset.

Section V. COUNTERATTACK ON THE GROUND

Experiences gained during their own air landings caused the Germans to regard attack as the only effective means of combating airborne operations. Their fight against Allied airborne operations demonstrated the wisdom of this rule. The Germans failed to crush the Allied invasion, not because this principle proved erroneous, but because the necessary forces were either lacking or could not be brought up quickly enough or because German counterattacks were not conducted properly. In many instances, however, these attacks did impede the progress of Allied airborne operations; at Arnhem they brought Allied operations to a complete standstill.

The most vulnerable period of any air landing is the interval between the jump and the assembling of the forces into organized units under a unified command. In order to exploit this weakness, German field service regulations stipulated that any unit within range of enemy troops which had landed from the air should immediately attack since every moment's delay meant an improvement in the situation for the enemy. This method proved to be fundamentally sound. It led to success whenever the enemy landed in small scattered groups or whenever the landing was effected in the midst or in the immediate vicinity of German reserves ready for action. But these tactics are not successful if the defending forces available for immediate action are too weak to defeat enemy troops vastly superior in number, or if the defenders are too far from the point of landing to be able to exploit the enemy's initial period of weakness. Then there is no longer any purpose in dissipating the defending forces in small isolated attacks or in doggedly fighting the enemy. It now becomes necessary to launch a systematic counterattack.

Speed in carrying out a counterattack against enemy airborne troops is essential, because it is certain that the enemy's fighting strength will be increased continuously by means of additional reinforcements brought in by air. In general, only motorized reserves are successful in arriving in time. If the enemy's air force succeeds, as it did in Normandy, in delaying the arrival of reserves, the chances for success dwindle. The elements which are nearest the enemy have the task of defending important terrain features against air-landed troops, maintaining contact with them, and determining the enemy situation through reconnaissance until all necessary arrangements for the counterattack have been made. The counterattack should be conducted under unified command and, as far as possible, launched as a converging attack from several sides and supported by the greatest possible number of heavy weapons, artillery, and tanks; it is directed against an enemy who is well prepared and whose weakness lies merely in that he may be troubled by lack of ammunition and in that his heavy weapons, in general, are inferior in number since he has not established contact with those elements of the invading force which are advancing on land. To prevent the enemy from establishing contact is therefore highly important. If this fails, the defender's chances for success are considerably less. There were no cases during World War II in which the Germans succeeded in annihilating airborne enemy troops after they had established contact with their forces on the ground.

The greatest stumbling block encountered by the Germans in combating Allied airborne operations in the West was the superiority of the Allied air force. German failure to eliminate this air force, or even to clear the skies temporarily, led to the most serious delays in bringing up reserves. The general scarcity of mobile reserves, combined with the fact that they were tied down elsewhere by order of the German High Command, led to the result that in Normany counterattacks were made too feebly, too late, or not at all. The success of the German counterattacks at Arnhem was due to the energetic action and unified command of Army Group B; the fortunate coincidence that two SS panzer divisions were in the immediate vicinity; the weather, which prevented Allied air intervention; and the resistance offered by the German troops at Nijmegen which prevented the prompt establishment of contact between Allied ground troops and airborne elements.

Section VI. COUNTERLANDING INTO THE ENEMY AIRHEAD

German specialists in airborne tactics (General Student and others) adhered to the theory that the best defense against an enemy air landing was the launching of airborne operations into the enemy airhead. However, no practical knowledge was gained concerning such operations. During World War II there was only one case in which air landings were effected from both sides in the same area and in quick succession. In 1943 in Sicily, south of Catania, British parachutists jumped into an area where, unknown to the British, German parachutists brought in by air to serve as reinforcements had also jumped a short while before. German reports at hand vary in their appraisal of this incident. One report mentions a complete victory gained by the British troops with heavy casualties among the German parachutists. Another report speaks of the annihilation of the majority of the British paratroopers. What actually happened was that one small British group did succeed in reaching its objective, the bridge at Primosole, but then lost it. Whether or not this occurred because of or in spite of dual airborne operations can hardly be determined without a more thorough investigation of facts. An air landing into an enemy airhead will always result in confusion on both sides. It will, of necessity, lead to chaotic hand-to-hand fighting, similar to the cavalry battles fought centuries ago, in which ultimately the tougher and more tenacious fighter will be victorious. The initial advantage is definitely gained by the opponent who is aware of the situation and jumps into the enemy airhead deliberately. If, in addition, he is supported from the outside by a concentrated thrust on the ground, it is quite likely that he will succeed in achieving a complete victory. The only question is whether, in the case of a large-scale airborne operation which definitely presupposes the air superiority of the attacker, the defender will be in any position to carry out an air landing. At night this might be conceivable. In any event, such a counterjump likewise requires preparations and is therefore possible only if the attacker lands in an area where the defender has taken such preparatory measures.

Section VII. AN APPRAISAL OF ALLIED AIR LANDINGS

During a war, the success of one side and the failure of the other are interrelated. In general, the success of the defender's measures can best be judged by the degree to which the attacker, as the active party, has been able to realize his goal. From this point of view the three major Allied airborne operations during 1944-45 will be briefly evaluated.

The Allied air landings in Normandy in June 1944 were carried out in close tactical collaboration with the amphibious operations. The Germans expected the air landings to take place farther inland, and to be aimed at more strategic objectives. Defensive measures were taken accordingly. The choice of landing areas for the over-all operations came as a surprise and, consequently, the defensive front was such that in comparison with other areas it was inadequately fortified and was held by weak German forces. The majority of the German reserve was committed elsewhere and was only reluctantly released for action.

Passive defense measures taken by the Germans did not influence the progress of the Allied airborne operations to any large extent. The first air landing, owing to an error in orientation, was dispersed far beyond the originally planned area. This caused the dissipation of initial German countermeasures. Isolated German successes were not able to prevent the over-all success of the air landing. Besides, since the drop zones covered a large area, it was difficult for the German command to quickly gain an accurate picture of the situation. This resulted in the erroneous commitment of the reserves and also had an adverse effect on the morale of the German troops. Because of the unmistakable air superiority of the enemy, it was impossible for the German countermeasurers to be executed rapidly enough. The German counterattacks were able to narrow the landing areas temporarily and to limited extent; they succeeded in preventing the troops which had landed from immediately taking the offensive. They also succeeded in temporarily placing the Allied airborne troops in critical situations.

The German reserves were almost completely tied down by the air landings, making it impossible to launch effective counterattacks against the amphibious assault. Consequently, the attackers were able to gain a foothold on the coast and, within a short time, to establish contact with the airborne elements. The tactical objective of establishing a bridgehead was thus accomplished despite German countermeasures.

The significant fact is that the air landings made it possible to substantially increase the number of forces which had been brought to the mainland during the first phase, thus augmenting the purely numerical superiority of the attacker over the defender.

It is open to question whether air landings with distinct concentration of forces on tactical objectives would have caused a more rapid collapse of the German over-all defense. Of course, the landings on the beaches would then have been more difficult. It also might have been possible to unify the German countermeasures against the invasion more effectively. The chances for greater victory would have involved a greater risk.

The air landings at Eindhoven, Nijmegen, and Arnhem in September 1944 were directed at breaking up the German front and paving the way for the British troops to reach the northern flank of the Ruhr area via the Meuse, the Waal, and the lower Rhine Rivers. The plan of attack offered the best chances of a major strategic victory. The operations also differed greatly from the Normandy landing in that they occurred during mobile warfare. Consequently, the Germans were unable to take defensive measures to the extent possible under conditions of position warfare. On the basis of intelligence reports, the Germans had anticipated enemy airborne operations. Furthermore, the commanders in the near-by home defense zones (*Wehrkreis* VI and *Luftgau* VI), as well as those in Holland, had made arrangements well in advance in order to be able to quickly form motorized auxiliary forces (so-called alert units) from home defense troops and occupation forces. These measures proved very effective, although the fighting strength of the alert units was necessarily limited.

In conformity with German principles, the air landings were attacked as soon as they were recognized. Two factors proved particularly helpful for the Germans. First, the air landing was not accompanied by any major attack by the Allied ground forces, but was supported only by a thrust on a narrow front launched by relatively weak armored spearheads, and was not followed by a heavier attack until the next day; secondly, the weather changed. Consequently, as early as the next day, the reinforcement and resupply of the airheads was considerably hampered and nearly ceased altogether for several days. At the same time the operations of the Allied air force against the German countermeasures, which in Normandy had caused so much damage, were greatly curtailed for some days.

The German counterattacks against the two southern airheads in the area of Eindhoven and south of Nijmegen neither managed to crush them completely nor prevented their joining forces with the advancing ground elements. However, the Germans repeatedly succeeded in causing critical situations which delayed the advance of the Allied ground forces. Specifically, they managed to hold the bridge at Nijmegen for another four days, thus preventing the enemy from establishing contact with the northernmost airheads at Arnhem.

At Arnhem, in the meantime, the counterattacks conducted under the unified command of Army Group B, whose operations staff was stationed there, had been successful. The two worn-out SS panzer divisions which by pure chance were still in the vicinity, and the above-mentioned alert units, whose fighting strength was negligible, were the only troops available at the time. Nevertheless, the airheads of the 1st British Airborne Division was narrowed continually, until it was finally annihilated with the exception of small portions which escaped to the southern banks of the lower Rhine River.

The German tactics had proved successful. Although they had not been able to prevent a deep penetration by the enemy, the Germans had managed to dispel the great danger of a strategic break-through, such as the Allies had planned. It was another six months before the Allies were able to launch an attack across the Rhine.

The Allied airborne operation at the Rhine, north of Wesel in March 1945, involved two airborne divisions. They were dropped directly into the river defense zone, operating in closest tactical collaboration with the ground troops which were launching an attack across the river. This air landing had been prepared with the greatest attention to detail and was supported not only by a large-scale commitment of air forces, totaling more than 8,500 combat planes in addition to over 2,000 transport planes, but also by the entire artillery on the western bank of the Rhine. It was practically a mass crossing of the river by air. The operation was a complete success for it was impossible to take any effective countermeasures. The German troops struck by the attack—worn-out divisions with limited fighting strength—defended their positions for only a short time before they were defeated. The only reserves available consisted of one training division whose troops had been widely dispersed to escape the incessant air attacks. This division was issued orders to launch a counterattack, and one regimental group did temporarily achieve a minor success against the landed airborne troops. The rest of the division was not committed at all, because enemy low-level planes completely wrecked all means of transportation.

Section VIII. REFLECTIONS ON THE ABSENCE OF RUSSIAN AIR LANDINGS

It is surprising that during World War II the USSR did not attempt any large-scale airborne operations. Although Soviet Russia was the first country in the world which during peacetime had experimented with landing troops by air and had organized special units for this purpose, its wartime operations were confined to the commitment of small units which were dropped back of the German front for the purpose of supporting partisan activities and which had no direct tactical or strategic effect. The reasons can only be surmised and might have been any or all of the following:

1. In 1941, when the Soviet Union entered the war, the Red Air Force was far inferior to the Luftwaffe. It is likely that the awareness of this inferiority persisted until the final stages of the war.

2. The Russians are primarily at home on the ground and are not in their element on the water or in the air.

3. In 1941 the parachute troops that had existed during peacetime may well have been expended in ground combat during the initial emergency. Later on, other parachute units were activated. Perhaps they lacked the necessary confidence or were considered too valuable to be risked in operations for which success was not assured. It is also possible that during the last phase of the war such operations simply were no longer regarded as necessary.

4. Marshal Tukhachevski was the originator of the Soviet parachute forces and after his removal the driving force in this new and untried field may well have been lacking.

Be that as it may, the fact that during World War II the Soviet armed forces did not carry out any large-scale airborne operations, such as were carried out by the Germans in Crete and by the Allies in Holland, should not lead to the false conclusion that the Soviet Union is not concerned with this problem or would fail to make use of this new arm during future military operations.

After finishing this study the author received additional information about an airborne operation carried out by the Russians late in the summer of 1943. Under cover of darkness, the Russians parachuted approximately three regiments into the area northwest of Kremenchug, about 25 miles behind the German front on the Dnepr. The exact date and place could not be given from memory. Only infantry forces without heavy weapons were dropped and they showed no initiative after the jump. Landing in small groups scattered over an area about 25 miles across, each group dug in on the spot, making no effort to contact other groups. Apparently they had no contact with their take-off base, and there were no simultaneous attacks by Russian ground forces across the Dnepr.

Within a few days the individual groups were mopped up with little difficulty at their separate landing places by German security formations and reserves. It was assumed that the Russian airborne troops would make their positions known to Russian airplanes by fires at night. The Germans therefore lit fires all along the river banks from Kremenchug to Kiev during the night following the jump. The Russians parachuted no further troops nor did they drop any supplies after the night of the landing. It is unknown whether a follow-up was intended or if it did not take place because of the uncertainty of the location of the landed forces brought about by the German deceptive measures.

The whole enterprise left the impression of inadequate preparation. Inadequate reconnaissance, mistakes in navigation during the approach and jump, lack of contact among the individual groups and between them and their base, as well as the complete passivity of the parachuted troops were the main deficiencies. The enterprise must be considered a complete failure. This may be why it remained so obscure that all German officers interviewed in connection with the original study, including General Student, General Blumentritt, and General Meindl (all officers with a comprehensive knowledge in this field), unanimously and independently stated that no large-scale airborne operations had been carried out by the Russians during World War II. As a result of investigation it was confirmed by a second informant that this Russian airborne operation actually took place at Kremenchug, but no further particulars could be procured.

Although this Russian airborne operation disclosed no new important experience in opposing airborne attacks, it seems appropriate to mention it if only for its singularity. Its complete failure may be a further reason, in addition to those mentioned above, for the absence of other large-scale Russian airborne operations in the course of the war. The impression prevails that tactically and technically the Russians could not meet the requirements of such an enterprise. Further reasons may be that the Russian soldier as a rule is not a good individual fighter but prefers to fight in mass formations, and that the junior Russian commanders lacked initiative and aggressiveness, two qualities that are basic requirements in a parachute officer.

The main effort of the Russian paratroopers during the war was without doubt in partisan warfare, an old method of combat that has always been favored by the Russians. In this field parachuting was widely exploited. However, this is a special subject having nothing to do with tactical airborne operations, and is therefore outside the province of this study.

CHAPTER 3

CONCLUSIONS

Section I. EVALUATION OF PAST AIRBORNE EXPERIENCE

In spite of rockets and atom bombs, it is still the possession of the land, the conquest of enemy territory, that will decide the issue in a war. The possession of the land is the visible sign of victory, and its occupation is a guarantee of the exercise of complete control. The occupying power definitely deprives the enemy of all chances of exploiting the territory with regard to natural resources, raw materials, industries, population, air bases, etc., while the occupier is able to utilize these for his own benefit and in the end force the enemy to surrender. The prerequisite, however, for the capture, the occupation, and the holding of a territory is the elimination of the enemy fighting forces which can defend the country and dispute its possession.

For a long time the most effective means of eliminating the enemy fighting forces seemed to be the method of envelopment, which is stressed particularly in the German theory of the art of war. An envelopment is directed at the enemy's weakest spot and cuts him off from his rear communications. During World War I the increasing effectiveness of weapons and the expansion of armies lessened the chances for large-scale envelopments and led to extended front lines with flanks anchored on impregnable points. The tactics of envelopment were replaced by the break-through, which during World War II was the objective of the mobile and combat-efficient panzer formations.

Airborne operations, carried out for the first time during World War II, point to a new trend. An air landing behind the enemy front is, after all, nothing but an envelopment by air, an envelopment executed in the third dimension. Herein lies its significance and an indication of the role it will play in future wars.

World War II has shown that airborne operations are practicable; furthermore, the results have proved that air landings are not one-time measures which owe their effectiveness exclusively to the element of surprise and then can no longer be applied. On the contrary, the events of World War II have demonstrated that it is extremely difficult for a defender to prevent or render ineffectual any airborne operations which are carried out with superior forces.

The airborne operations carried out during World War II still represent in every respect purely tactical measures taken in closest co-operaion with the ground forces. Strategic concepts rarely entered into the picture. Even the capture of an island represented an individual action of strictly limited scope.

The continued technical improvement of all types of aircraft since the end of the war with regard to speed, range, and carrying capacity makes it appear quite possible that the scope of airborne operations will also increase in proportion to the number of forces and weapons which can be employed. Even today, it is probably no longer utopian to think of air landings as large-scale envelopments or even, beyond that, as outflanking movements in the third dimension, which will no longer merely aim at attacking the enemy's position from the rear, but will force him to relinquish his position in order to form an inverted front against the attacking forces that have landed far behind his lines.

For the most part, such considerations are limited by technical factors. This study cannot determine what these limitations are and how they apply to the present or the future, if only for the reason that the author lacks the necessary technical information. Besides, at the present rapid rate of technical progress, today's daydreams may be accomplished facts by tomorrow. This report, therefore, merely represents an analysis of some of the problems involved in airborne operations and a general evaluation of the resulting possibilities.

Section II. LIMITATIONS OF AIRBORNE OPERATIONS

First of all, it should be remembered that airborne operations are governed by the same strategic and tactical principles that apply to any envelopment or flanking movement. A correct evaluation of the terrain and the time element, the ratio of friendly and enemy forces as well as the proper depth of attack in proportion to the available troops, the concentration of forces in a main effort and arrangements for containing the enemy at other points, the elements of surprise and deception—all have to be weighed and taken into account just as carefully as in ground operations. Consequently, they do not have to be discussed in further detail at this point.

The new element in airborne operations is the peculiarity of the approach via the third dimension, that is, by air. The accompanying difficulties as well as advantages should therefore be analyzed with particular care and must be taken into account in an evaluation of the above-mentioned factors.

In the main, this new method of attack by air gives rise to the following difficulties:

1. The forces employed for air landings are highly vulnerable while they are on the approach route. This necessitates control of the air

along the entire route, from the take-off points up to and including the landing area. Apart from other factors, the geographic limits of the area in which the attacker enjoys air supremacy determine the depth of a large-scale airborne operation.

2. An air landing, more so than any operation on the ground, is a thrust into unknown territory. The conventional means of reconnaissance and sources of information offer inadequate results and require a great deal of time. From the moment the airborne troops land, they face surprises against which they are not protected by advance reconnaissance and security measures and from which they are no longer able to escape. Consequently, every airborne operation involves a greater risk than ordinary ground combat, requires more time for preparation, and entails a distinct moment of weakness during the first phase of landing.

3. After the initial landing the fighting strength and mobility of airborne forces depend on their chances for resupply by air. It will no doubt be possible to improve the purely technical facilities available for this purpose. In this respect the military planners need not be afraid of asking too much from the men who are responsible for research and development. The really decisive factor is whether the military situation in the air permits the air transport of supplies. Just how far the attacker's air supremacy can be extended, not only in space but also in time, is a fundamentally important question. Another vital consideration is the time interval until contact with friendly ground troops can and must be established. The proper evaluation of these possibilities will always be the determining factor for the extent and scope of airborne operations and hence for the selection of suitable objectives as well. These difficulties are not insurmountable. They will be overcome by technical progress, organization and training of the forces, and proper tactical and strategic commitment, always of course within reasonable limits and with the necessary prerequisites.

4. However, there is one unalterable difficulty—the inflexibility of an airborne operation at the time of execution. Once the plan has been decided upon and the operation has been set into motion, the entire action necessarily has to unfold according to schedule. The only control the high command can still exercise is through the commitment of its reserves. The initiative exercised by intermediate and lower echelons, which in ordinary ground combat assures flexibility of adjustment to the existing situation and which in the German Army was particularly stressed as a vital combat requirement, is largely eliminated during airborne operations. It cannot begin to take effect until an attack is launched from the captured airhead. Only in part can these deficiencies be offset by careful and detailed

preparations, which take time, and by committing even greater quantities of troops and matériel, which again proves that airborne warfare is a "rich man's" weapon.

[Field Marshal Kesselring's comments on the inflexibility of airborne operations:

I do not agree that airborne operations are absolutely tied to a fixed schedule and are therefore too rigid in their execution. Naturally, an airborne operation executed according to plan will be assured the greatest probability of success. Should the situation require a sweeping change in plans, however, this can be carried out by signal communications from ground to air and between the flying formations. This will require the preparation of alternate plans and intensive training of the units. Formations on the approach flight can be recalled or can be ordered to land at previously designated alternate fields. This is less complicated in the case of later serials. In my opinion such changes can be carried out more easily in the air than on the ground. In land warfare, once large formations are committed in a certain direction toward a definite objective, major and minor changes involve equal difficulties. There is no reason why this should be any different in an airborne operation.]

Section III. ADVANTAGES OF AIRBORNE OPERATIONS

Despite the cost in men and matériel, airborne operations offer such outstanding advantages that no future belligerent with the necessary means at his disposal can be expected to forego using this combat method. The following are the main advantages:

1. The airborne operation makes it possible for the attacker to carry out a vertical envelopment or to outflank front lines or lines with protected flanks; it also enables him to surmount terrain obstacles which interfere with the movements of ground troops, such as wide rivers, channels, mountains, and deserts.

2. The airborne operation can be launched from the depth of the attacker's zone. It develops with extraordinary speed and offers remarkable opportunities for surprise attacks, with regard to time and place, and thus forestalls any countermeasures by the enemy.

3. The psychological effect of vertical envelopment is considerably greater than that produced by horizontal envelopment. It can affect the enemy command and troops solely by reason of its menace—the uncertainty of when and where an air landing might take place. The consequent effect on the population of the country, either positive or negative as the case may be, should also not be underestimated.

Section IV. REQUIREMENTS FOR SUCCESS

An armed force desiring to overcome the difficulties which arise from the use of airborne operations and seeking to make the most of the advantages offered by such operations should, in consideration of the statements made so far, arrive at the following conclusions:

1. The attacker's air force should be so strong that even at the beginning of the war it will either be wholly superior to the enemy, or, in fighting the enemy air force, will seriously weaken that force and thus pave the way for mastery of the air with regard to time and space.

2. It is necessary to have available a highly qualified specialized force for the execution of airborne operations. Air landings require tough fighters eager for action, an intensive and diversified training, the best kind of equipment, and ample air-transport space. It is advisable to recruit this specialized force from volunteers. Men who have been taken from the militia or conscript army and have received only brief training, might require an extended tour of active duty. Above all, however, this force should be activated in peacetime, not in cadres only but in full strength, since such a specialized force cannot be organized quickly. These requirements again demonstrate that airborne operations will always be something which only the "rich man" can afford.

3. Any planning for airborne operations on a large scale should include preparations for the movement by air of large ground units (divisions) to permit the prompt reinforcement of airborne troops after their initial landing. The necessary adjustments with regard to equipment and organization must be carefully considered and applied, and specialized gear must be at hand.

4. It should be realized that an airborne operation is as rapid in its execution as it is time consuming in its preparation and affords neither much freedom of maneuver nor a great deal of flexibility; it must be prepared well in advance. Once it has been set into motion, its direction and objective can no longer be changed. Even in peacetime it is therefore necessary to draw up blueprints for certain conceivable airborne operations, blueprints which are to be carefully modified on the basis of current information obtained in the course of actual hostilities. If this work has been done, the time required for preparation in each individual case can be considerably reduced. Only through foresighted preparatory work covering several likely situations is it at all possible to achieve a limited degree of flexibility in the execution of airborne operations.

5. Finally, it should also be mentioned that air landings, even more than any other operations, are dependent on the weather. The more territory an airborne operation is supposed to cover, the greater will

be the need for a long-range weather forecast system, which even during peacetime will have to be set up with an eye to functioning under such wartime limitations as the absence of weather data from enemy countries.

Section V. ANTIAIRBORNE DEFENSE

With regard to defense measures against airborne operations, the following conclusions may be drawn from this study:

1. The best method of defense is and always will be a strong air force.

2. The next requirement is a well-organized observation (radar) and warning system; it is essential to succeed in setting up this network quickly, even in a war of movement, and to adapt it to the fluctuating situations.

3. Local defense measures and preparations for all-around defense are increasingly important for rear elements. In addition, it will be necessary to establish clearly who, in the rear areas, will be in command of all forces which have to be committed in case of enemy air landings, and who will be responsible for making the necessary arrangements to this effect.

4. In an era of constantly growing possibilities for operations far behind the front lines, the need for prompt and forceful action against hostile air landings will eventually force any belligerent to scatter his strategic reserves over the whole of his communications zone, and even parts of the zone of the interior; he may also be compelled to hold large forces in readiness for the express purpose of defending his rear areas against long-range enemy airborne operations.

Section VI. FUTURE POSSIBILITIES

Future wars will offer far-reaching possibilities for the employment of airborne operations. The selection and scope of the objectives will always depend on the available forces (air force, airborne troops) and consequently will be a question of war potential. But the employment of airborne operations as a weapon in future wars also will depend on an early decision to make use of it, because air landings cannot be improvised, either in obtaining the necessary forces or in the technical aspects of the operation itself.

At the beginning of World War II, the strategic employment of armor completely changed the concepts of warfare carried over from World War I; it is quite conceivable that, at the beginning of a future war, the employment of large airborne units will play a similar role.

APPENDIX

NOTES ON GERMAN AIRBORNE OPERATIONS*

Section I. EQUIPMENT OF GERMAN PARACHUTE TROOPS

During the war, the weapons and equipment of German parachute troops did not differ essentially from those of the infantry. The paratroop automatic rifle, which used standard ammunition, was the only special type of small arms developed. It was adopted because the automatic rifle of the infantry did not use standard ammunition. In any paratroop operation the most harassing problem was the method of carrying ammunition. Since the rifle was attached to the man while jumping, the weapons containers, most of which after 1942 were transportable, became available for carrying ammunition. In 1944 a so-called ammunition vest for each man was introduced in some parachute units and proved successful.

Immediately after the Crete operation the paratroops had requested the construction of special midget tanks (*Lilliputpanzer*), which could be carried along on airborne operations, as well as special light weight portable antitank guns. Experiments were begun in 1942 on a two-man tank which could be transported in a large troop-carrying glider and which because of its shape was called a "turtle." Because of difficulties in the armament production program, the experiments were discontinued toward the end of 1942 before it was possible to form a definite opinion on the usefulness of the model. In any case, it seems to have met the Army's three requirements of low silhouette, high speed, and great cross-country mobility as fully as possible.

In 1942 the paratroops were given a 48-mm./42-mm. antitank gun with tapered bore and solid projectile as a special weapon for antitank fighting instead of the impractical 37-mm. antitank gun, which was difficult to transport. The gun did not prove especially successful in Africa against the heavy British tanks and its production was discontinued in 1943. At the same time the so-called *Panzerwurfmine* (magnetic antitank hand grenade) was introduced as a special weapon for fighting tanks at close range, but it was soon replaced by the *Panzerfaust* (recoilless antitank grenade and launcher, both expend-

---
*By Col. Freiherr von der Heydte.

able). In autumn 1944 the German engineer Schardien was working on a new close-range antitank device for airborne use which would have been easier to transport than the *Panzerfaust;* he was probably unable to complete his experiments.

Some of the paratroop units used the so-called *Einstossflammenwerfer* (one-thrust flame thrower) of the SS, which was considerably better adapted to paratroop use than the Army flame thrower.

The greatest headache for the German paratroop command was the lack of artillery in support of infantry fighting. The German paratroops were equipped with the excellent 75-mm. and 105-mm. airborne recoilless guns; both had short barrels and carriages made of light metal alloy. In suitable terrain the 75-mm. gun could be easily drawn by two men, and its elevation was the same as that of the 37-mm. antitank gun of the Army. The maximum range was 3,850 yards for the 75-mm. gun and 9,000 yards for the 105-mm. gun. Both had the following disadvantages:

a. A large amount of smoke and fumes was generated, and the flash toward the rear was visible at night for a great distance.

b. They could be used only as flat-trajectory weapons. Attempts to use the airborne recoilless guns as high-angle weapons were not satisfactory. Moreover, in an airborne operation it was seldom possible to carry along the necessary amount of ammunition or have it brought up later. Thus, as a rule, only important point targets could be attacked with single rounds, generally from an exposed fighting position.

Besides these weapons, 150-mm. rocket projectiles were used in the Crete operation. They were fired from wooden carrying crates, which also served as aerial delivery containers. These rockets did not prove successful; because of their high degree of dispersion they were suitable only for use against area targets and in salvo fire. However, the quantity of projectiles needed for such a purpose could not be transported on an airborne operation, and a Ju–52 (German troop carrier) could carry and drop only four projectiles at a time.

The parachute troops were generally forced to rely on Army signal equipment which, to be sure, was available to them in far greater quantities than it was to any other units. The "Dora" and "Friedrich" radio sets proved very successful in German air landing operations. Ever since 1942 the troops had repeatedly requested in addition a small, portable short-range radio set for communicating between companies, but no such set was introduced. Several units, therefore, made use of captured American equipment. For the projected Malta operation of one parachute battalion, the engineering firm of Siemens-Halske supplied a portable radio set for maintaining contact with the base. It had a definite range of 180 miles, could be operated without interruption for six hours, and could easily be carried by one man.

Carrier pigeons and messenger dogs proved very successful in airborne operations; the former for communicating with the base, the latter for communication within the company or from company to battalion. The dogs, equipped with a parachute that was automatically disconnected from the harness after landing, generally jumped very willingly and without accidents. In 1942 a signal cartridge, protected against misuse by the enemy by a special contrivance, was introduced on an experimental basis. However, the experiment was very soon discontinued.

Section II. GERMAN EMPLOYMENT OF TROOP-CARRIER UNITS

In Holland in 1940, the Germans came to realize the disadvantage of the parachute commander's inability to exercise any direct authority over the troop-carrier units; the two were co-ordinated, but neither was subordinate to the other. Consequently, before carrying out the Crete operation the troop-carrier units were incorporated into the parachute corps, of which they constituted an integral part under a special Luftwaffe officer (*Fliegerfuehrer*). This arrangement did not last long. The operations in Russia and North Africa required the concentration of all air transport services directly under the commander in chief of the Luftwaffe to assure the prompt execution of any air transport operations which might become necessary, and only in the rarest cases did this involve carrying paratroops. As a result the training of troop-carrier units was also reorganized. The pilots were then trained to fly in "main bodies" (*Pulk*) or in a "stream of bombers" (*Bomberstrom*), that is, in irregular formations which were always three dimensional. However, it is impossible to drop parachutists from the *Pulk* or *Bomberstrom* formations; dropping parachutists requires a regular flight in formation at a uniform altitude, that is, a two-dimensional flight. The close flight order of the conventional heavy bomber formation, with its effective cross fire on all sides, is desirable for approach flights across hostile territory. It provides defense against enemy fighter planes and can be maintained until shortly before the parachute or airplane landings. If there is a probability of strong antiaircraft fire, the plane-to-plane and group-to-group spacing will have to be increased. For such tactics, intensive training of the troop-carrier pilots will be necessary, especially in the proper deployment preparatory to parachute drops.

Losses during the attack on Leros in the autumn of 1943 are said to have occurred mainly because the troop carriers did not fly in regular formation and at the same altitude; during the air landing in the Ardennes in December 1944 it proved a fatal mistake that the troop-carrier units were no longer accustomed to flying in regular formation. The experience gained both at Leros and in the Ardennes has shown that it is essential for a troop-carrier unit which is to drop parachutists to be trained to do this work, since a good part of the success of an airborne operation depends on flying in regular close formation at the same altitude. It is obvious that the necessary training in formation flying is best achieved if the troop-carrier units are subordinated to the command of airborne troops from the very first. Up to the end of the war the German paratroop command continued to demand that it be given permanent control over the troop-carrier units, but this demand remained unfulfilled. That the troop-carrier units must be subordinate to the airborne command at least for the duration of an operation is clear to everyone. The fallacy of letting nonspecialists make decisions in such matters was demonstrated in the less than brilliant direction of the Leros operation by a naval officer (the Commanding Admiral, Aegean). Likewise the Ardennes operation, which was prepared by an Air officer (the Air Force Commander, West), and carried out by an Army officer (the Commanding General, Sixth SS Panzer Army); one knew as little about an airborne operation and its difficulties as did the other.

Although the problem of co-operation between the airborne command and the command of the troop-carrier units was solved at least temporarily during the Crete operation, the co-operation, or lack of it, between the individual airborne unit and the individual troop-carrier squadron continued to be the greatest cause of complaint by the airborne troops during the entire war. At best, the individual airborne battalion commander became personally acquainted with the commander of the transport group which flew his battalion only 2 or 3 days before the operation; as a rule, the individual soldier did not establish any contact with the flying crew of the machine which had to transport him. There was no mutual understanding of peculiarities, capabilities, and shortcomings. The 2d Battalion of the 1st Paratroop Regiment was almost completely annihilated in Crete because the battalion commander of the airborne troops greatly overestimated the flying ability of the troop-carrier unit which was to carry his men, whereas the commander of the troop-carrier force, on the other hand, did not understand the extremely elaborate plan of attack of the airborne commander, who was a complete stranger to him. In former times one would not require a cavalry regiment to carry out an attack when its men had only been given a short course in riding but had not been issued any horses until the night before the attack.

Next to the pilot, the most important man in the flying crew was the airborne combat observer, or, as the troops called him, the jumpmaster (*Absetzer*), that is, the man who gave the signal to jump. The jumpmaster should be an extremely well-trained observer and bombardier. In the German airborne forces he was just the opposite. The jumpmasters were not taken from the flying personnel of the Luftwaffe but from the airborne troops; from time to time, the various parachute units had to release one or two men for training as jumpmasters, and with the inherent selfishness of any unit they naturally did not release their best men but rather their worst, who for some reason or other could no longer be used as paratroopers. If this reason was a combat injury, the men might still have served their purpose, but more often than not the reason was lack of personal courage or intelligence. The jumpmasters selected in this negative manner were trained at a jumpmasters' school by instructors who had been detailed from the flying personnel of the Luftwaffe. The Luftwaffe did not release its best instructors for this purpose. After this deficient training the jumpmaster waited in some troop-carrier unit, like the fifth wheel on a wagon, until he was needed for an airborne operation, meanwhile forgetting what little he had learned at the school. For, like bombing or firing a weapon, dropping paratroops is a matter of practice, of constant uninterrupted practice. The German jumpmasters were completely lacking in this practice. In almost every airborne operation the consequences were disastrous. During the Crete operation at least one platoon of each battalion was landed incorrectly; at Maleme entire companies were dropped into the sea because the jumpmasters—out of fear, as the paratroopers afterwards claimed—had given the signal too early; during the Ardennes operation one company was dropped on the Rhine north of Bonn instead of south of Eupen, and the majority of the signal platoon of that company was dropped south of Monschau directly in front of the German lines.

Only on two occasions, the operation near Eben Emael in 1940 and the projected operation of dive-gliders against Malta in 1942, were paratroopers and troop-carrier units brought together for orientation and joint training for a considerable period prior to the operations. In both cases co-operation was excellent.

Section III. TECHNIQUE AND TACTICS OF AIRBORNE OPERATIONS

The German airborne forces carried out two kinds of airborne landings—the parachute operation and the troop-carrying glider operation. After 1942, as a general principle, the parachute troops were trained in both kinds of airborne landings so that such units could be used at any time either in parachute or in glider operations, according to the tactical and terrain requirements.

The Ju-52 and He-111 were available as troop-carrier planes. From the Ju-52 the jump was made through the door, from the He-111 through a jump hatch. Jumping from the door proved more successful since the men were more willing to jump out of the door than through the hatch in the floor of the plane and because the landings were effected at considerably smaller time intervals. In a well-trained unit 13 men could leave the plane in not more than eight seconds. With the planes moving at a speed of 100 to 120 miles per hour and at an altitude of about 330 feet (100 meters), there would be a distance of about 25 yards between men immediately after landing; that is, the group reached the ground in a fairly compact formation and could be immediately assembled by the unit commander if the terrain offered a reasonable degree of visibility.

The jumping altitude was generally a little more than 330 feet. As commander of the instruction battalion, the author carried out tests at lower jump altitudes; at a jump altitude of 200 feet, the lowest that was reached, casualties through jumping injuries rose to an average of 20 percent. As soon as the jumping altitude was raised much in excess of 330 feet, the ground dispersion of the group increased. According to experience gained in the instruction battalion, a jumping altitude of about 670 feet resulted in an average dispersion of a group of 13 men amounting to 900 yards in depth and over 200 yards in width, about twice the average dispersion attained with a jumping altitude of 330 feet.

Jump casualties as well as dispersion depended largely on the velocity of surface wind, the determining of which was, or should have been, one of the most important special tasks of the combat reconnaissance directly preceding any landing operation. In general, German paratroops were only able to jump with a surface wind not over 14 miles per hour. Operations with a surface wind of greater velocity resulted in many jump casualties and often delayed the assembly of the landed troops for hours. The relatively large losses from jump casualties during the airborne operation against the island of Leros in the autumn of 1943 must be attributed entirely to the high surface wind. During the airborne operation in the Ardennes in December 1944 a surface wind of 36 miles per hour caused heavy casualties. Of the elements of one airborne unit which could still be assembled after the jump, more than 10 percent were injured in jumping, which did not, however, prevent most of them from taking part in the fighting a few hours later.

The German parachute fell short of requirements. It caused an excessive swinging motion in gusty weather, it was hard to control, and too much time was required to get out of the harness. Too much importance was probably attached to safety in jumping and too little to suitability for combat operations. The casualties which were sustained from enemy action because the soldier was unable to free himself from his harness quickly enough were far greater than the casualties which might have been caused by carelessness in opening the single-fastening harness release in the air. During the Ardennes operation I myself made an experimental jump with a captured Russian triangular parachute which despite strong gusts and a surface wind of 36 miles per hour brought me to earth with almost no oscillation. At the time, I still had my left arm in a temporary splint. In that wind it would have been impossible to jump with a German parachute when one's arm was in a splint.

Too much importance was attached to the rigging of parachutes; valuable training time and time prior to an operation was lost because every man had to rig his own parachute. In my regiment I made the experiment of introducing a parachute maintenance platoon which rigged the parachutes for the entire regiment. The results were very good. Jumping experiments with unrigged parachutes have shown that in an emergency it is sufficient to make two air-resistance folds (*Luftschlagfalten*) and that much of the complicated packing procedure was mere fussiness.

Since heavy casualties had been sustained in Crete because the paratroopers could not reach their weapon containers or because they had to leave cover in order to unpack the containers, after 1942 regular training was given in jumping with the weapons attached to the soldier. This proved very successful. The soldier carried any one of the following items on his person: pistol, submachine gun, rifle, light machine gun, boxes of ammunition for machine guns and medium mortars, machine gun carriage, or short intrenching tool. In addition, each of the following items of equipment was dropped successfully by auxiliary parachute attached to a soldier: medium mortar barrel, medium mortar base plate, and "Dora" and "Friedrich" radio set.

At first the German airborne troops placed too much emphasis on the nature of the terrain at the drop point. Practical experiences during the war showed that well-trained troops can make combat jumps anywhere, except in terrain without cover where enemy fire is likely to engage the paratroops immediately after landing. Moreover, rocky terrain is particularly unfavorable. A landing in woods presents no difficulties in jumping technique, although it makes assembly very difficult after the jump. During training, German paratroopers frequently jumped into wooded areas, but in combat only once—in the Ardennes operation in 1944. It is also possible to land among groups of houses, that is, on roofs. Of course, this requires special training and equipment. The paratrooper must be able to cling to the roof with the aid of grappling hooks and quickly cut an opening in the roof so that he can make his way into the house.

Regular training in night jumping first began in 1942 and soon produced good results. After 1943 the requirements for the award of the paratrooper's insignia after the completion of training included at least one jump at night. In combat, night jumps were made by the Germans on only one occasion, during the Ardennes operation. Night jumping presented two main difficulties—locating the drop point, and establishing contact after jumping. For locating the drop point which had to be reached accurately by every airplane within a few hundred yards, the radio-control procedure customary in night bombing operations was not satisfactory since it was too inaccurate and led to many errors. In practice, therefore, the Germans made use of two other procedures to supplement rather than replace radio control: a technical radio device, the so-called radio buoy (*Funkboje*) and the incendiary-bomb field (*Brandbombenfeld*). The radio buoy was a shockproof, short-range radio transmitter packed in an aerial delivery container, which was released over the drop zone by a pathfinder plane flying ahead of the troop-carrier unit and then automatically gave each troop carrier the signal for dropping as soon as the aircraft had flown to within a certain area. The experiments with the radio buoy, which were carried out after 1943, had not yet been concluded to complete satisfaction by the end of the war. Therefore, during the Ardennes operation the author made use of the simpler method, the incendiary-bomb field. Two fields of incendiary bombs were laid out on the ground about one mile apart by a pathfinder plane of the troop-carrier unit, and the landing unit was to be dropped halfway between these two incendiary-bomb fields. This was not successful in the Ardennes operation, not because of any defects in the procedure but rather because of the strong American ground defenses and the unbelievably bad training of the flying personnel of the two troop-carrier units engaged in the mission. Co-operation with pathfinders in night jumping requires the most accurate timing. Because of incorrect wind data, the pathfinders in the Ardennes operation arrived at the drop zone almost a quarter of an hour too early. In this way not only was the American air defense warned in advance, but the last transport planes were no longer guided and had to drop their men blindly.

In order to establish contact on the ground after a night jump the Germans generally used acoustical signals, such as bird calls and croaking of frogs, in preference to optical communication. Radio was used only to establish contact between company and company and between company and battalion. In the summer of 1942 experiments were made with jumps in bad weather and in fog, but without satisfactory results.

The Germans distinguished between two kinds of operation with troop-carrying gliders—gliding flight and diving flight. Great results were expected of the latter in particular. The same craft were used for both operations, either the small DFS which could carry 10 men with light equipment or the larger Go, a glider with a double tail assembly which could carry a load equivalent to one German 75-mm. antitank gun, including a two-man gun crew. The type of tow plane and method of towing were the same for both kinds of operation. The He–111 was mostly used as a towing aircraft. The Ju–87 was best adapted for diving operations. In general, the cable tow was used to pull gliders; experiments with the rigid tow produced debatable results.

German gliders were specially equipped for diving operations. A "ribbon" parachute was provided as a diving brake. This consisted of several strips between which the air could pass. The glider pilot released this parachute by hand the moment the craft tipped downward. The take-off wheels were thrown off after the start, and the glider landed on a broad runner wrapped with barbed wire to increase the braking effect. This runner was directly behind the center of gravity of the glider. On some gliders designed for special types of operation there was a strong barbed hook, similar to an anchor, which dug into the ground during the landing. Finally, certain gliders were also provided with a braking rocket in the nose which could be automatically or manually ignited at the moment of landing and gave the landing machine a strong backward thrust. In some experiments a glider thus equipped was brought to a halt on a landing strip only 35 yards long.

An approach altitude of about 13,000 feet seemed particularly favorable for diving operations. The glider was released 20 miles before the objective and reached the diving point in a gliding flight. As a rule, the diving angle was 70° to 80°, the diving speed around 125 miles per hour, the altitude at which the pilot had to pull out of the dive about 800 feet. In diving, the glider could elude strong ground defense by spinning for a short time or by frequently changing its diving angle, diving by steps (*Treppensturz*) as it was called. In training pilots for diving operations the greatest difficulty was experienced in teaching them to make an accurate spot landing, in which under certain circumstances even a few yards might be important, and to recognize the right moment for pulling out of the dive. To my knowledge, it was only once that the possibilities offered by dive-gliders were put to use in combat. In 1943 seven 75-mm. antitank guns were dropped into the citadel of Velikie Luki, which was surrounded by the Russians, by using Go's as dive-gliders. In connection with the projected paratroop operation against Malta in 1942, six hours before the parachute jump, a battalion under my command was supposed to land by means of dive-gliders among the British antiaircraft positions on the south coast of the island and to eliminate the British ground defense. Over a period of months the Malta operation was prepared down to the smallest detail, and during that time the parachute troops practiced on mock-ups of these positions.

Toward the end of the war the German airborne forces clearly defined three methods of attacking an objective:
1. Jumping or landing on top of the objective;
2. Jumping or landing near the objective;
3. Jumping or landing at a distance from the objective.

According to German views, jumping or landing on top of the objective is the method primarily suited for attacking an objective which is relatively small and specially fortified against a ground attack. The Germans considered the troop-carrying dive-glider best suited for such an operation. Examples of landing on top of the objective are the capture of Fort Eben Emael north of Liège in 1940, the unsuccessful attack by elements of the airborne assault regiment (*Sturmregiment*) in gliders against British antiaircraft positions near Khania on the island of Crete, and the jump by my combat group at the crossroads north of Mont Rigi, in the Eifel Mountains of western Germany.

Jumping near the objective is the preferred method used for the capture of a bridge or an airfield. Here the general rule is that the men jump toward the objective from all sides, so that the target to be attacked lies, so to speak, in the center of a bell-shaped formation of descending troopers. Examples of jumping near the objective are the capture of the Moordijk bridges in 1940, the capture of the Waalhafen airfield near Rotterdam in 1940, and the capture of the Maleme airfield in Crete in 1941. While, in spite of the bravest fighting, the British did not succeed in capturing the Arnhem bridge from the air in 1944, this was probably in large part because they did not jump near their objective but at a considerable distance from it.

According to German views, jumping at a distance from the objective should be resorted to chiefly when the objective is so large that it can only be reduced by slow, systematic infantry attack; inch by inch, so to speak. Whereas in jumping near the objective it is a basic rule that the attack must be made from several sides, in jumping at a distance from the objective the attack on the ground must be launched on a deep, narrow front from one direction. An example of this method was presented in the attack by the 3d Parachute Regiment against the city of Khania on the island of Crete in 1941. To be sure, it is doubtful whether such an operation would today be carried out in the same manner. Since it has been determined that it is possible for paratroopers to attack buildings from the air, the best method of attack for the purpose of capturing a village might be a combination of jumping on top of the objective and jumping near the objective rather than the procedure used in Crete in 1941; evidently the easiest way to capture a village should be from within. To date, of course, no practical experiences are available on this subject.

As a result of their experiences the Germans distinguished between two ways of dropping a parachute force: landing all elements of a unit in the same area; landing all elements of a unit at the same time.

To accomplish the landing of all elements in the same area, the troop carriers approach the drop zone in a deep, narrow formation and all paratroopers jump into the same small area. For a battalion of 600 men, a landing area measuring about 900 yards in diameter and a landing time of about 30 minutes will be normal. According to German experience, this method of landing a unit is to be used especially at night, in jumping into woods or a village or other areas with low visibility, as well as in jumping at a distance from the objective. It was, for example, the mistake of the 3d Battalion of the 3d Parachute Regiment in Crete that it failed to choose this type of landing. Its heavy casualties can in part be attributed to this fact.

If all elements of a unit are to be landed at the same time, the troop carriers make their approach in wide formation to various drop zones situated close to each other and all paratroopers jump, as nearly as possible, at the same time. In such an operation, the landing area for a battalion of 600 men will usually measure at least 2,000 yards in diameter, with a landing time of less than 15 minutes. According to German experience, this method of landing a unit is to be especially recommended when jumping into terrain which offers little cover, as well as when jumping near the objective. In Crete, the 2d Battalion of the 1st Parachute Regiment made the mistake of landing at a number of widely separated small drop points at very long time intervals. As a result of the delay, the battalion was almost completely wiped out. It can be stated as a general rule that the larger the landing area, the less time should be spent in the dropping operation. Anyone who is careless with respect to time and space will be annihilated.

[Field Marshall Kesselring's comments on the three methods of attacking an objective (see page 54):

First method.—Airborne landings into an area which is strongly defended against air attack can succeed only when there is absolute surprise. To be sure, the effect of weapons against parachutes in the air is generally overestimated. However, every landing harbors within itself a pronounced element of weakness which increases while troops are under the defensive fire of the enemy and which may lead to disaster during the very first moments of ground combat. The examples of Arnhem (1944) and Sicily (1943) speak only too eloquently for this; such examples will occur again and again. The attack against Fort Eben Emael can be considered as an example to the contrary. The study of this attack will enable one to recognize the possibilities and limitations of such operations.

Second method.—The prerequisites for a landing near the objective are correctly described. Such landings, however, should be planned so that they are not subject to the disadvantages which occur when jumping directly into the objective. When one has to reckon with strong antiaircraft defenses, a success costing few casualties can generally be achieved only through surprise. Gliders are superior to parachutists because of their soundless approach.

Third method.—In large-scale operations it will be the rule to jump at a point some distance away from the objective. One should not belittle the advantage of landing, assembling, and organizing troops in an area which is out of danger! The factor of surprise is still retained to a greater or lesser extent according to the time of day or night, the weather conditions, and the terrain. A combination of landings into and near the objective may be advisable or necessary for tactical reasons or for deception, in order to scatter the enemy fire. The same purpose may be achieved by launching diversionary attacks when landing at some distance.]

www.ingramcontent.com/pod-product-compliance
Ingram Content Group UK Ltd.
Pitfield, Milton Keynes, MK11 3LW, UK
UKHW041423180426
11947UKWH00007B/260